The Dominie Collection of Traditional Tales for Young Readers

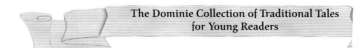

The Three Little Pigs

Retold by Alan Trussell-Cullen

Illustrated by Denise Elliott

DOMINIE PRESS
Pearson Learning Group

Once upon a time, there were three little pigs. They all lived with their mother. One day their mother said, "It's time you built a house of your own."

So the three little pigs said good-bye to their mother, and off they went.

The first little pig met a man with a load of straw.

"Straw is just what I need to build a house," said the first little pig. So he bought the straw from the man and built a house for himself.

4

The second little pig met a man with a load of sticks. "Sticks are just what I need to build a house," said the second little pig. So he bought the sticks from the man and built a house for himself.

The third little pig met a man with a load of bricks.
"Bricks are just what I need to build a house," said
the third little pig. So he bought the bricks from the
man and built a house for himself.

The next day, the big bad wolf came into the little pigs' neighborhood.

He went up to the house of straw and knocked on the door.
"Little pig! Little pig! Let me come in!" said the wolf.
The little pig said, "No! No! No! By the hair on my chinny-chin chin, I will not let you in!"

The wolf was angry. "Then I will huff! And I will puff! And I will blow your house down!" he said.

And he huffed. And he puffed. And he *did* blow the house down!

The frightened little pig ran down the road to the house made of sticks.

The big bad wolf followed him. He knocked on the door.
"Little pigs! Little pigs! Let me come in!" said the wolf.
The little pigs said, "No! No! No! By the hair on our
chinny-chin chins, we will not let you in!"

The wolf was even angrier. "Then I will huff! And I will puff! And I will blow your house down!" he said.

And he huffed. And he puffed. And he *did* blow the house down!

The little pigs were very frightened. They ran down the road to the house made of bricks.

The big bad wolf followed them. He knocked on the door.

"Little pigs! Little pigs! Let me come in!" said the wolf.

The little pigs said, "No! No! No! By the hair on our chinny-chin chins, we will not let you in!"

The wolf was furious! "Then I will huff! And I will puff! And I will blow your house down!" he said.

And he huffed! And he puffed!

And he puffed! And he huffed!

But he could not blow the house down!

The wolf was even more furious! He climbed up onto the roof and shouted down the chimney, "Little pigs! Little pigs! I am coming down the chimney to eat you up!"

Now at the time, the third pig was cooking
a pot of soup. When the wolf came down the
chimney, he fell straight into the hot soup.

"Help!" cried the wolf.

He jumped out of the soup and ran out of the house.

And the three little pigs never saw him again.

"A house made of bricks is better than a house made of straw or a house made of sticks!" said the three little pigs. And they all lived together happily ever after.

My family treads lightly on the lands of the Bunurong and Wurundjeri peoples of the Kulin Nation. We recognise their continuing connection to land, waters and culture, and pay our respects to their Elders – past and present.

Salad for Days

Alice Zaslavsky

Salad for Days

Alice Zaslavsky

murdoch books

Sydney | London

*For my family,
and for yours*

Contents

Well, hello there ...

The notion that you don't win friends with salad has haunted me and my fellow vegelantes (vigorous vegetable-lovers) ever since Homer Simpson used this fateful line in an ep about Lisa going vegetarian. It became a chant, then a meme, and it's been echoing in my ears for decades. Which may seem like no big deal, until you consider that the consumption rates of salad — and of vegetables in general — are in dire straits.

True, the '90s — when that episode of *The Simpsons* aired — were not kind to salads. Limp lettuce, fat-free dressings, too many sundried tomatoes … it's no wonder that people weren't lining up to give salad a rap. But times have changed, as has the definition of what a salad can be. No longer merely a bowl of leaves, Salad 2.0 can be just about anything you want it to be. Cooked or raw veg, greens, grains, carbs, nuts, seeds, cheese, fruit — bring it on. As far as I'm concerned, if you're talking at least two types of produce, intentionally combined, with a dressing of some kind, it's a salad!

So I put to you a new paradigm: you DO win friends with salad … when you cart a kaleidoscopic container-load to a friend's barbecue; when you plonk a bowl of zippy greens down alongside grand mains to cut through and cleanse the palate; when you toss pantry ingredients together for lazy bowl-food on the couch. Use this book of salads as a seasonal reference guide or a daily recipe roster. It's organised for warmer days (spring through summer) and cooler (yep, autumn and winter). The warmer-day salads make the best of juicy, sun-drenched produce to restore and refresh, particularly on those days so hot you don't feel like cooking, while the cooler ones will coat your *kischkes* and give heartier brown food (so great!) a counterpoint on the table, so that you finish the meal feeling better than when you started. Eating with the seasons is easy when salad is involved, since so much of it is about knowing how to treat the veg in the first place, and often doing less rather than more.

And you can eat these salads for breakfast, lunch and dinner. Some of them, like the Relaxed chopped salad (page 80), are a mainstay on our breakfast table; others, like the Honeyed butternut risoni (page 163) are perfect for lunch *al desko*; and of course there are myriad inspirational platters and bowls for when you're asked to bring-a-plate (or pot-luck, depending where you are in the world).

Colours abound here, because as we learn more about the benefits of bioactives contained within each hue of an ingredient, the notion of 'eating the rainbow' becomes more than just a bumper sticker. Indeed, thinking about getting your colours in is far easier and more enjoyable than thinking in serves or micronutrients. We eat with our eyes, and the more colours we can let them feast on, the more appetising the meal. Some combinations just work: like the red and green of summer produce, pinks and paler greens of spring, amber hues of autumn and deeper jewel tones of winter.

Mother Nature puts those palettes before us because they're the ingredients we need at that time of year — whether we're healing sunburnt shoulders with the lycopene of olive-oiled tomatoes, supporting our eye health with Vitamin A from root veg and capsicums as the light begins to fade earlier through autumn, or warding off cold season with the Vitamin C in deep-green leafies. Juicy, raw vegetables in spring and summer make way for grounding spices and cooked veg in the cooler months when digestive energy is best conserved.

The more colours you pack into each meal, the better for you. I've thought about combinations of colours and flavours that make sense in my Kodachrome brain, but the beauty of these salads is that each can stand alone or join the party … and the guest list is up to you.

Food should make you feel good: when you buy it (or grow it); when you cook it with a sense of confidence and playfulness; when you serve it to family and friends; when you eat it; and, especially after the meal is done, when the lushness of fresh ingredients and the vim that's gone into the preparation and assembly leaves you vibrating with life. Salads are perfect for making friends happy too, because they're easy enough for even beginner cooks to whip up. If you're hosting a big get-together, flick a pic of a salad you like the look of to each of your guests to lighten the load, and give everyone a sense of collegiality before the meal's even begun.

The fact of the matter is, you *can* win friends with salad, and it's *very* ready to make friends with you. ◂

HOW TO USE THIS BOOK

Effort-to-return is one reason I love salad-making. It's really more about assembly than too much cooking, and the magic comes in the sum of the parts. Those parts are laid out clearly throughout: recipes will tell you what the final bits and bobs are, because they're like the accessories that bring it all together, and what each salad is friends with (though the beauty is that they really all can be mixed and matched).

Most of the recipes are designed to feed four to six people, but will usually keep overnight if you're a smaller household. I'll often tell you how they'll perform as 'prep-aheads' in the intros.

There's also a dressings index (see page 20) and, because there are 80-odd different ones to choose from, you can find one to suit any mood and lift every spirit.

Speaking of spirits, keep an eye out for a few bonus ways to shake up spare ingredients into cocktails, shrubs and bonus bits, because I'm all about making the most of it: produce and life!

Simple steps to stick the landing

1. SEASONED PROFESSIONAL

When a recipe says 'season to taste', the 'to taste' bit is usually referring to salt, because there's a remarkable variation in the saltiness of salts available. So it pays to pay attention to the type of salt recommended — particularly in a recipe where it's used with relatively few other ingredients, such as salads. You'll notice I call for salt flakes in these recipes, but even flaky salt can vary, so don't take my word for it — taste the dressing and correct if needed before calling it a day.

My favourite salt is a pink lake salt from Down Under, but anything flaky, where the jaggy surface area shimmers across the finished product like snowflakes, is the direction to take. If you have fine table salt, quarter the salt amount given and taste judiciously. Do consider investing in flaky salt if you can (online retailers will often run sales on products like this, which is a handy time to stock up, because salt won't go 'off'); it makes a massive difference to the end result — not just to the flavour but also visually and texturally — and is one of the bigger bang-for-buck swaps you can make.

2. CRACK ON!

Some spices you can get away with buying pre-ground, but black pepper isn't one of them. Grinding peppercorns to order is a revelation, not only for the fizzy tingle but also the floral aroma, which will make you sneeze if you whiff too close. I think it adds to pepper's intoxicating appeal. If a recipe gives you a measurement, pop the base of the grinder into your palm and crack the pepper in, then syphon into a measuring spoon to measure. A quarter of a teaspoon is plenty for a dressing for 4–6. For recipes that say 'a good crack', it's very much an eye and feel job. I have a black peppercorn grinder set at 'fairly coarse' (about the halfway mark) for adding fresh into salads, and a white peppercorn one set to 'fine' for dishes where it gets cooked in (white pepper's a little too hay-shed on the nose for me). I use green peppercorns in one of the recipes here (see page 60); you can buy them in brine and they will last for AGES in the fridge — terrific for serving with any sliced fruit. Pink peppercorns are great for finishing a dish if you've got them handy (though they'll need to be crushed with a mortar and pestle as they're too soft and juicy through the middle for a grinder).

3. OIL YOU NEED IS LOVE

If you're feeling overwhelmed by the prospect of 80-odd dressings' worth of ingredients, I'm gonna let you in on a little secret. Pretty much any salad can just as easily be dressed with extra virgin olive oil and a bit of S&P. It's what turns a platter of cut veg from crudités to chopped salad, and sliced tomatoes on a plate to one of the most stupendous ways to celebrate summer. Extra virgin olive oils labelled 'fruity' or 'mild' are best for dressings, as they'll meld with the rest of the ingredients rather than dominating. I do like to splash out (pun intended) on a small bottle of something more herbaceous and bitter for occasional 'finishing' (this is when you grab the bottle in your hand, hold it over the salad and give it one last flick of the wrist for dramatic effect, like you're Jackson Pollock). For neutral oils, I'll give a sense of which direction to take with my 'preference' in the recipes, but aim for the mildest flavour and aroma you can find.

4. ACID TRIP

When balancing a dressing, or looking for that *je ne sais quoi* in a salad, the answer is probably 'acid'. Whether that's a squirt of citrus or splash of vinegar, this is the element that cuts through richness and leaves your mouth puckering and poised for another bite. You really can't go past lemons for a cheap and cheerful kick of sourness. Don't forget to zest the lemon before you juice it, and consider using the peel for a more intense flavour (see the recipe on page 219). Limes are 'saltier' than lemons, so swapping one for one requires adjusting the seasoning a little. One lemon usually contains 3–4 tablespoons of juice, while a lime contains about half that. For maximum juiceage, roll your lemon or lime across the bench or zap for 20 seconds in the microwave before juicing. A white wine vinegar is the simplest and purest acid but can be a little sharp, depending on the brand. Buy the best you can afford, because the cost is reflective of time in the barrel. If you're on a budget, fake the barrel time with a pinch of sugar and five minutes of supervised burbling to reduce and intensify, or by adding a little honey or maple syrup into the dressing if it's not already there.

Pickled and preserved vegetables provide pucker and serve a digestive function too, so it's no accident that pickles mean a lot to me. Check out the Pickle Party on page 13 for inspo: my favourite is dill pickles, of course. Condiments vary wildly too. On the following page is a snap of the brands and bottles that we used in this book; keep an eye out for them in your pantry and at the shops. And, as always, taste, taste, taste.

5. HIT REFRESH

As the great philosopher Derek Zoolander once said, 'Moisture is the essence of wetness, and wetness is the essence of beauty.' As soon as produce is picked, it starts to lose moisture, exacerbated further by transportation, handling and the arctic aridness of refrigeration. But all is not lost! The more porous your veg, the easier it is to reinvigorate. Send lacklustre lettuce and crusty celery to the day-spa in the form of a dip in a bowl of water, the colder the better. 'Refreshing', as it's technically called, is also excellent for creating curly spring onion slices, crisping up radish and fennel, and giving soft herbs an extra spring in the frond. If you're in a hurry, ice cubes to chill the water will accelerate the effect. You can slide the whole day-spa back into the fridge if you've got other things to get on with. If you're prepping ahead, cover the prepped veg with damp paper towel to maintain its juiciness, just like they do in the restaurants.

6. SPIN IT TO WIN IT

I feel like I'm in the pocket of Big Spinner with the amount of times these cop a mention, but if you want to eat more salad, get a salad spinner. I know I've just told you to hydrate your herbiage, but if you don't dry off the exterior when ready to use, the dressing's just going to slip right off. It may feel like just an extra gadget, but I use my salad spinner to save time, because it's so easy to soak, drain and spin all in the same vessel. If you're short on space, soak in a bowl and whack into a tea towel to whirl about (just do this outside so you don't flail everything off the shelves).

7. A CUT ABOVE

Here's a rule of thumb worth remembering: the smaller your slices, the shorter to table-time. What that means is that if you're serving the salad right away, and not planning on leftovers, cut the veg smaller for the dressing to permeate quickest. Ergo, if you're travelling a distance, chunkier shapes will hold better. Follow the contours of the vegetable if you want to highlight the beauty of a fennel bulb or capsicum bell, or cut everything uniformly to celebrate a colour explosion. One sharp chef's knife is best for processing the veg (the sharper it is, the less likely it'll bounce off harder veg), along with a serrated paring knife for smaller tasks and chopping softer tricksters like tomatoes. If your knife skills are a work-in-progress, outsource: use a food processor or mandolin for slicing your slaws (watch fingers!) and grab a julienne peeler for thinly slicing veg like zucchini or carrots.

8. ALWAYS ADD AN ALLIUM

As far as I'm concerned, a salad needs some amount of allium to round out the flavour, whether that's a white salad onion for the mildest hit, a Spanish red for its colour and sweetness, or a bog-standard brown for zing. Spring onion (the long green one) is easy to slice and scatter, with a mellow, syrupy flavour. Shallots are somewhere between spring onion and onion proper, and I particularly like the way adding acid to them makes them blush. In most of the recipes in this book, shallots can be interchanged between the squat brown/yellow shallot (French eschalot), the Thai red and the elongated banana shallot (though the last is best for fine slicing with the grain, as you'll get nice long strips).

When cutting onions for salad, stick with following the grain if you want the crunch of the onion to come through, or against if you'd prefer it to be more about the flavour than the texture. If you've allium-averse folk in your midst, serve diced or sliced onion on the side so people can help themselves (it's worth doing the same with other potentially divisive ingredients like coriander). You'll notice I'm very generous with the garlic, which you're welcome to ease off on if you're not equally enthused, or do as I do and pop a garlic powder shaker on the table beside the salt, pepper and extra virgin olive oil, so people can treat themselves.

9. FAT IS FLAVOUR

If you've eaters in your midst who say that salad isn't satisfying, then I know just what they've been lacking: fat. Whether that's in cheese form, or avocado, extra virgin olive oil, nuts or some kind of creamy bed or dressing, fat is the secret to satiety.

10. TOSSING CAUTION

If you've ever looked at a schmicko restaurant salad and wondered how they managed to dress it so evenly and serve it without a smidgen of schmear, it's time to start double-bowling. Toss your salad in a large bowl (the bigger the better) then turn it out onto a serving platter or clean bowl to serve. A good pair of tongs (silicone-tipped, spring-loaded) will help if you're not adept at the flick-n-toss, and will ensure that you get right down to the bottom, like you're turning compost.

11. BOWLS & PLATTERS ELEGANZA

To up your salad-serving game, invest in some beautiful bowls and platters. No need to break the bank, mind you — thrift shops and flea markets are your best friends, because big bulky bowls are the first to hit the deck when people decide to Spark Joy. If creating a new serving-ware wardrobe, do as stylist extraordinaire Kirsten Jenkins did for this book: choose a colourway, then stick to the family, whether that's broody darks that make bright veg pop, muted neutrals or bright whites. When choosing whether something needs a bowl or a platter, think about the way you want your diners to see the salad — if it's a vertical job that looks best from the side, then platter up! If it's extra juicy, or needs more tossing at the table, give yourself some higher sides to keep the table from wearing more than it bargained for.

Dress it up

Dressing up, or down, is one of life's great joys — in fashion and in the kitchen! Here's a wardrobe of options for any mood or occasion. Try combining one from each category (along with its corresponding salad, of course) for a coordinated tablescape with range. Three to four salads are plenty for a table of four to six diners. And if in doubt, do as Coco Chanel might, and take one dish off the shopping list before you leave the house.

Spicy & funky

Zippy & zesty

Rich & creamy

Bright & light

Crunchy bits

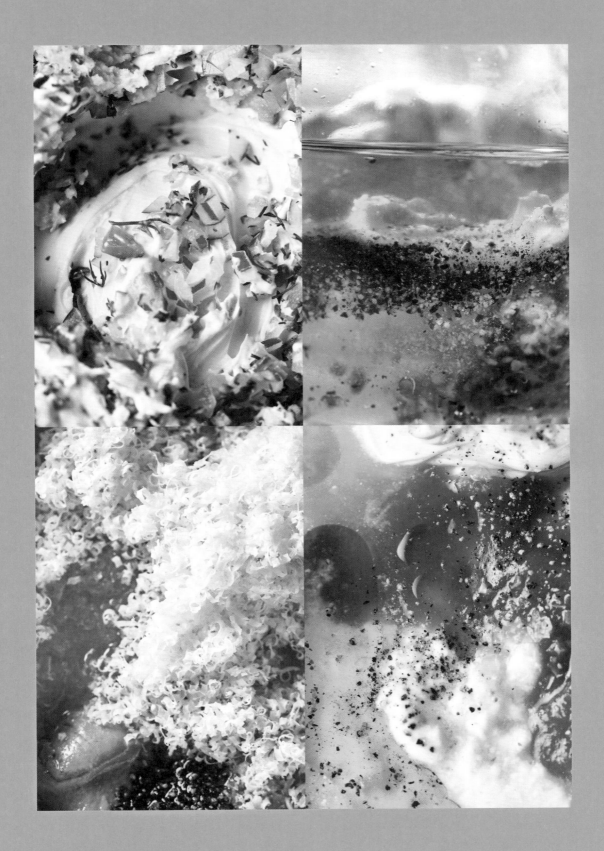

Warmer *Days*

I'm starting out the way I wish you to continue: with something practical AND conceptual. Three elements: one creamy, one crunchy and veg in a variety of colours! The zucchini flowers are nice to have, not a necessity: slice finely just before serving, remembering to take the stamen (middle) out first. PG (parsley and garlic) paste is one of the first search terms that comes up alongside my name, because of how popular it's been as a flavour bomb. You can toss it through a salad like this, use it as a marinade, even spread it on your toasties. Make double the PG paste and give the Calamari and shell pasta salad (see page 133) a whirl.

Sautéed squash *and* zucchini *with* pangrattato

To make the pangrattato, blitz together the parsley, lemon zest, garlic and olive oil in a food processor to form a verdant green paste. Heat the butter in a large frying pan over medium heat and toss in the breadcrumbs, along with half of the PG paste, stirring about until the breadcrumbs turn golden and the garlic aroma is unbearably irresistible. Transfer the pangrattato to a bowl and set aside. Loosen the remaining PG paste with the reserved lemon juice and set aside.

Wipe out the pan, then place over medium heat and add a third of your squash and zucchini bits to the dry pan. When they're golden brown on all sides, transfer to a plate. Repeat with the rest of the zucchini and squash until browned, then return it all to the pan, splash in the oil, butter and garlic, and toss about to coat. Turn off the heat, and stir in the reserved PG paste. Taste and season with salt and pepper.

Schmear the stracciatella on the base of a platter or shallow bowl. Tumble the squash and zucchini over the top. Finish with a drizzle of extra olive oil, then crumble the pangrattato over. Scatter with basil leaves and shredded zucchini flowers, if using.

6 patty pan (baby yellow) squash, cut into 5 mm (¼ inch) discs

6 baby zucchini (courgettes), cut into 5 mm (¼ inch) discs

1 zucchini, about 200 g (7 oz), cut into 1 cm (⅜ inch) jaunty pieces

4 variegated zucchini, cut into 5 mm (¼ inch) discs

3 tablespoons olive oil, plus extra to drizzle

50 g (1¾ oz) butter

2 garlic cloves, finely grated

300 g (10½ oz) stracciatella cheese

PG PASTE PANKO PANGRATTATO

½ bunch parsley, leaves and stalks roughly chopped

Zest of ½ lemon, juice reserved

5 garlic cloves

¼ cup (60 ml) extra virgin olive oil

25 g (1 oz) butter

1 cup (60 g) panko breadcrumbs

FINAL BITS & BOBS

½ cup basil leaves

6 zucchini flowers, finely shredded (optional)

FRIENDS WITH

Triple cherry Caprese p47, Calamari and shell pasta salad p133

Rooties – such as carrots and daikon – are one veg group that really respond to a gadget. Whether you're peeling them into ribbons with a speed peeler, shredding with a mandolin or julienne peeler, spiralising or grating on a box grater or food processor attachment, their fibrous bonds help to maintain structural integrity, while allowing more dressing to penetrate into their naturally sweet middles. Beware: these gadgets are SHARP! Use the base of your palm to grip and push the carrot rather than your fingertips, and when in doubt, save the rest for a chef's snack.

3 ways *with* shredded carrots & daikon

Carrot & daikon with sesame dressing

Shred the carrots and daikon.

In a small bowl, mix together the remaining ingredients, stirring until the sugar dissolves.

Toss the dressing together with the veg and set aside for 5–10 minutes for the dressing to have an influence, sprinkling with sesame seeds before serving.

Carrot & daikon with dill pickle mayo

Shred the carrots, daikon and pickle.

Mix together garlic, salt, mayo and 2 tablespoons of the reserved pickle juice.

Toss carrots, daikon and pickle through the dressing and set aside for 5 minutes to relax into itself before serving.

Vietnamese carrot & daikon quickle (**quick pickle**)

Shred the carrots and daikon.

If serving right away, pop them into a heatproof bowl. If planning on making it stretch, put them into a clean, sterilised jar with a tight-fitting lid.

In a small saucepan, boil ½ cup (125 ml) water together with the sugar and salt. Remove from the heat and pour in the vinegar, fish sauce and chilli, then quickly pour over the carrot and daikon to cover.

Leave to quickle for 10 minutes if serving right away, or pop the lid on and leave to cool before refrigerating and using in sandwich fillings and snack spreads for up to a month.

CARROT & DAIKON WITH SESAME DRESSING

2 carrots

1 daikon

1 spring onion (scallion), finely sliced

¼ cup (60 ml) neutral oil

1 tablespoon sesame oil

1 tablespoon rice wine vinegar

1 pinch sugar

1 teaspoon salt flakes

1 tablespoon toasted sesame seeds

CARROT & DAIKON WITH DILL PICKLE MAYO

2 carrots

1 daikon

1 large dill pickle, juice reserved

1–2 garlic cloves, minced

1 teaspoon salt flakes

¼ cup (30 g) Kewpie mayonnaise

VIETNAMESE CARROT & DAIKON QUICKLE

2 carrots

1 daikon

¼ cup (55 g) sugar

3 teaspoons salt flakes

1 cup (250 ml) rice wine vinegar

1 tablespoon fish sauce

1 long red chilli, finely sliced

FRIENDS WITH

Charred & smashed zucchini with labneh and chilli oil p75

SESAME DRESSING

DILL PICKLE MAYO

VIETNAMESE QUICKLE

This is a brill barbecue bring-a-plate, because you can prep ahead. Wash and spin the cos, chop and pop it into a paper towel-lined container for transport, along with the sliced spring onion and picked coriander. Boil the corn up to a day ahead. Once you toss the salad, the corn breaks up but it looks so dramatic arranged as sheets, which are best achieved by laying the corn on its side and shearing. The paprika–chilli mayo makes an excellent chip-dipper too. Turn it planty by using vegan mayo and holding the cheese.

Charred corn, cos *and* tomatoes *with* paprika–chilli mayo

2–3 baby cos (romaine) lettuces, trimmed

4 corncobs, husks and silks removed, halved horizontally

1 tablespoon extra virgin olive oil

400 g (14 oz) baby truss tomatoes (sugarplum), halved

PAPRIKA–CHILLI MAYO

½ cup (120 g) whole egg mayonnaise

¼ cup (60 ml) extra virgin olive oil

2 garlic cloves, minced

Juice of 1 lemon (about 3 tablespoons)

2 tablespoons sherry vinegar

¼ teaspoon chilli flakes

¼ teaspoon sweet paprika, plus extra to finish

¼ teaspoon salt flakes

FINAL BITS & BOBS

2 spring onions (scallions), finely sliced on the bias

½ bunch coriander (cilantro), washed, rinsed and halved (if super long)

50 g (1¾ oz) manchego cheese

Lemon cheeks

Slice the cos lettuce into 4–6 wedges, keeping them attached at the stem as much as possible. Pop into cold water to refresh and dislodge any grit.

Bring a large saucepan of water to the boil, add the corn and set the timer for 3 minutes. Drain and set aside until ready to char.

In a small bowl, whisk together all of the paprika–chilli mayo ingredients. Taste and season with additional salt and pepper if need be. Set aside.

Heat a grill plate or barbecue to smoking hot. Toss the corn in the olive oil, then place it on the hot grill and char on all sides for 10–15 minutes, weighing it down with something weighty (like a heavy frying pan) if you're in a hurry. When corn has sufficiently dramatic blackened bits, place flat on a board and slice the kernels off in slabs. Keep the skinned cobs as chef snacks to gnaw on while you get everything else organised.

Spin dry the cos lettuce and coarsely chop into 1.5 cm (½ inch) chunks against the grain. Scatter over a serving platter and top with the tomato halves and slabs of corn kernels. Drizzle with the paprika–chilli mayo, then top with spring onion and coriander leaf tendrils, along with puffs of finely grated manchego and a pinch of extra paprika.

Serve with lemon cheeks on the side.

FRIENDS WITH

Squashed squash on yoghurty lemon dressing p34

Come midsummer when tomatoes are aromatic enough to whack your nostrils at the shop door, there really is little else to do with them than eat and enjoy. Sniff the stems, gently tweak the torso for a hint of give, and eyeball the most vibrant, glossy hue. Tomatoes are best when salted about 10 minutes before serving, giving the salt flakes time to start to season the toms without producing too many tomato tears. A pinch of sugar tricks the tastebuds into thinking these are the ripest tomatoes of the season (something useful to note for cooked tomato sauces, too). If you can't find milk kefir, use buttermilk instead, or milk with a squirt of lemon juice for acidity.

Twinkling tomatoes *with* milk kefir dressing

Arrange the tomato slices artfully on a platter, tessellating and filling gaps with smaller slices.

Ten minutes before serving, sprinkle liberally with salt flakes, plenty of pepper and the sugar, if using.

While you wait, plonk the bruised garlic into the olive oil to gently infuse. To make the milk kefir dressing, mash the feta through the kefir with a fork. Loosen with a little more kefir or a splash of milk if it's a bit too chunky.

Drizzle tomatoes liberally with dressing and infused olive oil just before serving (holding any stray bits of garlic) and scatter with dill fronds. Season with more pepper and a scant pinch of salt flakes, from a height.

500 g (1 lb 2 oz) assorted tomatoes (all different kinds welcome), thinly sliced against the grain

Salt flakes and freshly cracked black pepper

1 teeny pinch sugar (optional but excellent)

1 garlic clove, bruised

¼ cup (60 ml) extra virgin olive oil

MILK KEFIR DRESSING

50 g (1¾ oz) crumbly feta

100 ml (3½ fl oz) milk kefir, plus extra for loosening

FINAL BITS & BOBS

Dill fronds

FRIENDS WITH

Grilled cos wedges with anchovy aïoli p112

If you're looking for a recipe that's surprisingly set and forget, then you've struck gold here. By the time the patty pan squash has charred up enough to squash, you've sliced and cured and forked to completion. I must say that the drama of everything in varying shades of gold and burnt umber is quite arresting at the table, but if you're finding it hard to source some squash, zucchini will also work. The yoghurty dressing yield is generous, so if you've got leftovers, consider swirling it through some sliced cucumbers tomorrow. If you've got dukkah in the pantry, feel free to deploy this here: I've left it out because it's already enough to ask you to pop out for preserved lemon.

Squashed squash *on* yoghurty lemon dressing

Heat a barbecue or heavy-based frying pan and char about two-thirds of the squashes on all sides (as you would an eggplant). Thinly slice the remaining squashes vertically, following the shape of the squash, toss with the brine from the preserved lemons and the sugar, and set aside for 10 minutes to infuse.

If this is the first time you're using preserved lemon, it's the pith and flesh that are especially bitter, so scrape these off with a sharp knife or teaspoon before finely chopping the rind. Combine all the dressing ingredients in a small bowl, mix well and set aside.

Smash the charred squash a little until the creamy innards show.

Smooth the dressing over the bottom of the serving plate. Arrange the smashed and brine-cured squash over the top along with the capsicum, and drizzle with extra olive oil, finishing with pine nuts, sesame seeds, mint and a grind of pepper to serve.

1 kg (2 lb 4 oz) patty pan (baby yellow) squash

1 teaspoon brine from preserved lemons (see dressing)

1 pinch sugar

1 yellow capsicum (pepper), deseeded, sliced thinly with the grain

PRESERVED LEMON DRESSING

1 tablespoon finely chopped preserved lemon rind

250 g (9 oz) natural yoghurt

1–2 garlic cloves, minced

Juice and zest of 1 lemon

1 teaspoon salt flakes

¼ teaspoon freshly ground black pepper

2 tablespoons extra virgin olive oil, plus extra for serving

FINAL BITS & BOBS

¼ cup (40 g) toasted pine nuts

1 tablespoon toasted sesame seeds

¼ cup mint leaves, finely shredded

FRIENDS WITH

Charred corn, cos and tomatoes with paprika—chilli mayo p31, 'Pita lid on it' fattoush p102

I've found myself eating more beans since learning that high bean consumption is one of the uniting factors across the world's longest-living cultures. I've chosen cannellini and green beans here, but you could easily use up whatever tins of beans are in the pantry, or fresh beans too – from broadies to yellow beans. You can use any kind of shallot – even white or red onion – as you want it to be a hum of allium rather than a hit. If your salad is travelling, bring the dressing in a jar and toss just before serving: it'll help the tomato and parsley hold their shape better and keep the beans from yellowing.

Long & short beans *with* very sharp vinaigrette

To make the vinaigrette, trim the woody ends off the parsley stems, then finely slice (if your stems are all too woody, finely slice a ¼ cup's worth of leaves instead). In a large bowl, whisk the vinegar, mustard, garlic and oil together, then add the sugar, salt flakes and pepper. Stir in the chopped parsley and sliced shallots. Taste and set aside until the beans are ready to rock.

Bring a medium saucepan of well-salted water to the boil. While you wait, top the green beans and slice in half on a deep diagonal, or use a bean splitter if you've got one in the drawer. Once the water is at the boil, chuck the green beans in for 2 minutes or until bright green and tender.

Meanwhile, drain the cannellini beans in a heatproof colander, then drain the green beans through the white beans to slightly heat them through. Shake off any remaining moisture and dump the lot into a mixing bowl, along with the cherry tomatoes and parsley leaves, then toss the vinaigrette through while everything's still warm.

Transfer onto a serving platter and serve warm right away, or pop into the fridge if you'd prefer to serve it chilled.

500 g (1 lb 2 oz) green beans

400 g (14 oz) tin cannellini beans

250 g (9 oz) tricolour cherry tomatoes, jauntily quartered

½ bunch parsley, leaves picked, stems reserved for dressing

VERY SHARP VINAIGRETTE

¼ cup parsley stems

2 tablespoons white wine vinegar

1 tablespoon dijon mustard

1 garlic clove, bruised

¼ cup (60 ml) extra virgin olive oil

½ teaspoon caster (superfine) sugar

½ teaspoon salt flakes

¼ teaspoon freshly ground pepper

2 banana shallots (see page 17), finely sliced

FRIENDS WITH

Tomato tonnato with crispy capers p41

CHARRED CORN, COS AND
TOMATOES (PAGE 31)

LONG & SHORT BEANS
(PAGE 36)

RELAXED CHOPPED SALAD
(PAGE 80)

The natural sweetness of tomatoes sings even brighter when juxtaposed with salty stuff like capers and tinned fish. Larger tomatoes can be quite meaty, which is why this pesco version of the Italian classic *vitello tonnato* totally works. The tomato slices soak up the creamy tuna dressing and make for a sensational lighter option for lunch or any night of the week. Fry some extra capers and pop them into a jar for sprinkling over any creamy salad that's missing something; their brininess makes them the ideal swapping candidate for anchovies for planty eaters or the anchovy-averse.

Tomato tonnato *with* crispy capers

2–3 tablespoons lilliput capers in salt, rinsed and drained well

3 tablespoons extra virgin olive oil

8–10 heirloom tomatoes (oxheart or other knobbly looking varieties most welcome), about 1.5 kg (3 lb 5 oz)

Handful of baby rocket (arugula), washed and spun

2 teaspoons aged balsamic vinegar

TONNATO CREAM

2 eggs

185 g (6½ oz) tin or jar of tuna in olive oil

1 teaspoon dijon mustard

Zest and juice of 1 lemon

1 garlic clove

¼ teaspoon each salt flakes and freshly cracked black pepper

¼ cup (60 ml) neutral oil (grapeseed is my pick)

FINAL BITS & BOBS

40 g (1½ oz) aged parmesan cheese, shaved

Freshly cracked pepper

To make the tonnato cream, bring a small saucepan of water to the boil. Add eggs and boil for 5 minutes. Run under cold water to cool, then peel. Blitz peeled eggs with tuna (including the olive oil), mustard, lemon, garlic, salt, pepper and neutral oil to form a fluffy, creamy consistency.

Heat well-dried capers in the olive oil on medium-high heat for 4–6 minutes until they begin to change colour and open their petals. Drain, reserving the olive oil.

Slice the tomatoes horizontally to 5 mm (¼ inch) thick, using a sharp serrated knife.

Pour tonnato cream over the base of a large platter, smoothing as you go. Arrange tomato slices on top across the surface, as you would vitello or carpaccio. Scatter the rocket over the tomatoes. Pour reserved caper oil into a small shallow bowl, then pour the balsamic in.

Just before serving, swirl the two together until a polka-dot pattern emerges. Drizzle polka-dot dressing over the top of the platter. Sprinkle capers about the place, then the shaved parmesan.

Finish with a final crack of pepper.

FRIENDS WITH

Long & short beans with very sharp vinaigrette p36

It would be remiss of me to collate a book of great salads without including a nod to the classics, though when it comes to canonical combos like this one, we can often get stuck in our ways. The surprise here is the stone fruit, which pops with sour–sweetness to elevate the lot. If this is a step too far for you, leave it out. The herbed feta is a Greek gift that keeps on giving: drama on delivery, and it turns the lot greener once you stir. If your telegraph cucumber's seeds aren't too fibrous, feel free to zebra peel (taking off half the skin in lengthways stripes) without scooping out the guts.

Greek-ish salad *with* nectarines

To make the honey–oregano dressing, whisk the garlic, honey, vinegar, lemon zest and juice, mustard, salt and the fresh and dried oregano together in a large bowl. Pour in the olive oil and whisk together to emulsify.

If the kalamata olives are with-pit and you'd prefer that they weren't (this is totally personal preference: not pitting saves time, pitting saves a trip to the dentist!) arrange the olives in batches on the chopping board and use the base of an olive oil bottle to squash them and release the pip. You can also squash them one by one with your thumb and index finger if you're up for a meditative task.

To make the herbed feta, squash the chopped herbs together to form a fuzzy green bed. Drizzle the olive oil onto the feta, then press the feta block into the herbs on all sides, so that it looks like it's had a run-in with the lawnmower.

Just before serving, add the prepared ingredients – the olives, onion, capsicum, cucumber, tomato and nectarine – to the dressing in the bowl and toss well to coat.

Transfer into a serving bowl, then prop the slab of herbed feta on top, finishing with some extra olive oil and the reserved pretty leaves, scattered from a height, to finish.

200 g (7 oz) juicy kalamata olives, drained

1 red onion, halved and finely sliced

2 red capsicums (peppers), deseeded and finely sliced into half moons

1 telegraph cucumber, zebra peeled and gutted, cut into 1 cm (⅜ inch) chunks

5 sweet truss tomatoes, about 500 g (1 lb 2 oz), cut into quarters

2 firm sweet free-stone nectarines, stoned and cut into fine wedges

HONEY–OREGANO DRESSING

1 garlic clove, minced

1 tablespoon runny honey

1 tablespoon red wine vinegar

1 teaspoon finely grated lemon zest

¼ cup (60 ml) lemon juice

2 teaspoons dijon mustard

½ teaspoon salt flakes

1 tablespoon finely chopped fresh oregano

½ teaspoon dried Greek oregano

¼ cup (60 ml) extra virgin olive oil

HERBED FETA

2 tablespoons finely chopped mint, reserving some whole leaves to garnish

¼ cup finely chopped parsley, reserving smaller whole leaves to garnish

1 tablespoon extra virgin olive oil, plus extra for serving

100 g (3½ oz) Greek feta, drained and chilled on paper towel in the fridge

FRIENDS WITH

Surf club salad p106

What's keeping you from making more spud salads? Is it potato-choice paralysis? Most greengrocers and supermarkets will kindly point you in the right direction with signage these days, but if you're still stuck, steam! Indirect, gentle heating is perfect for controlling the firmness of the final result, and for keeping edges crisper for contrast with the creamy dressing. Speaking of 'crisper', radishes are an ideal candidate for refreshing (see page 16) to have them at their best, and if you want the curliest spring onions, don't skimp on the soak time. This salad will last 2–3 days in the fridge.

Radish & potato salad *with* creamy tarragon dressing

Cut potatoes into roughly 1.5 cm (½ inch) chunks. Steam for 15–20 minutes until fork-tender but still firm, and leave to cool a little.

Meanwhile, get onto preparing the rest of the ingredients.

Set up 2 medium bowls of cold water (one for soaking, the other for refreshing). Remove any radish bindings (such as string or elastics) and place the whole bunch of radishes into one of the bowls, swishing about to release the grit. Slice the radishes into quarters and drop them into the other bowl of clean water. This may seem a tedious task, but trust me, the juicy crunch is well worth the effort, and it's harder to explain than to execute.

Finely slice the spring onions and drop into the bowl of clean water, along with the radish quarters.

Pull the prettiest leaves off the radish bunch (the middle leaves and a few of the smaller ones per radish) and pop back into the bowl with the radish quarters.

To make the dressing, whisk the vinegar, mustard, sugar, salt and pepper together in a large mixing bowl, add yoghurt and the olive oil, then fold the tarragon through. Taste and season again with salt and pepper.

Pour the spring onion, radish leaves and the radish quarters into a sieve or salad spinner, and spin or shake off any excess moisture. Combine the spring onion, radish quarters, still-warm potatoes and walnuts in the bowl with the dressing, tossing to coat.

Wipe your serving bowl with the bruised garlic clove, then tumble the potato mixture in, along with the radish tops. Finish with a flourish of extra olive oil.

4–6 red-skinned waxy potatoes, about 850 g (1 lb 14 oz)

1 bunch radishes, about 250 g (9 oz)

4 spring onions (scallions)

⅓ cup (40 g) shelled walnuts

CREAMY TARRAGON DRESSING

2 tablespoons white wine vinegar

1 heaped tablespoon seeded mustard

½ teaspoon sugar (optional)

1 teaspoon salt flakes

½ teaspoon cracked black pepper

½ cup (130 g) natural yoghurt

2 tablespoons extra virgin olive oil, plus extra for serving

2 heaped tablespoons finely chopped tarragon

FINAL BITS & BOBS

1 garlic clove, bruised

FRIENDS WITH

Asparagus and radish salad with caper vinaigrette p126

How lucky are we Down Under that the best baubles Mother Nature provides are at *their* best just in time for the festive season? I've chosen to halve and pit the cherries, but it's worth using a cherry pitter if you'd rather keep them whole. Letting the oil sit in the food processor allows the sediment to drop to the bottom, so you'll spend less time straining in the end, and leaving the pine nuts to sit in the smoking hot pan is a good way of toasting them just right without coming back to burnt nuts. It's all quite meditative, really – which is a good circuit-breaker when you've got a lot on your plate.

Triple cherry Caprese *with* bright basil oil

500 g (1 lb 2 oz) cherry tomatoes, halved

300 g (10½ oz) big firm cherries, halved and stoned

220 g (7¾ oz) cherry bocconcini, drained

BRIGHT BASIL OIL

½ cup loosely packed picked parsley leaves, reserving the prettiest ones for garnish

1 cup baby spinach leaves

1 cup tightly packed picked basil leaves, reserving the prettiest ones for garnish

½ cup (125 ml) neutral oil (grapeseed is my pick here)

½ cup (125 ml) extra virgin olive oil

FINAL BITS & BOBS

¼ cup (40 g) pine nuts

Salt flakes and freshly cracked pepper

For the bright basil oil, bring a medium saucepan of water to the boil. Fill a medium bowl with cold water and ice cubes and set it to the side. Once the water in the pan has come to the boil, chuck the parsley and baby spinach leaves into the water to blanch, then scoop them out right away and transfer into the iced water to lock in the colour. Leave for a few minutes. When cool, strain and squeeze out excess water from the leaves.

Put the blanched leaves, fresh basil and the oils into a food processor or blender. Blend on high for about 3–4 minutes until smooth and the oil turns a very rich green.

Once blended, let it sit in the food processor for 5 minutes. Pop a clean kitchen cloth or muslin in a fine mesh sieve over a medium bowl or jug. Pour in the bright green oil to strain and help catch the leaf residue. Strain gently – be patient!

Heat a heavy-based frying pan until smoking. Turn off the heat and put in the pine nuts, giving them the occasional toss and letting the residual heat cook them until golden.

Just before serving, toss the tomatoes and cherries together with 3 tablespoons of the bright basil oil and then transfer onto a serving platter.

Dot bocconcini artfully around the place. Garnish with pine nuts and reserved basil and parsley leaves.

Finish with a final drizzle of bright basil oil, a crack of pepper and a sprinkle of salt flakes.

FRIENDS WITH

Bistro bouquet with mignonette dressing p111

Larb is one of Laos's most famous edible exports, and though it's usually associated with minced meat, the idea of 'flesh' can be expanded upon to fleshy veg like eggplant. If you don't have palm sugar, there's no need to rush out for it: use maple syrup or brown sugar instead. You can also use any kind of shallots here, but the banana shallots are great because you can get nice uniform strips for quickling when sliced with the grain. Slice against the grain if you're using the squat ones. Watermelon radishes are nice to have, but they've such a short season, so if you can't find them, just use the regular kind of radish for crunch. This larb has some heat to it, but won't blow your head off the way some like to larb. If you're a heat-seeker, you know what to do.

Eggplant larb *with* quickled & fried shallots

Dice eggplant into 1 cm (⅜ inch) cubes (no need to peel), then pop into a colander, sprinkle with salt and set aside for 15 minutes to *schvitz* (that's sweat).

For the crispy shallots, pop half of the shallots into the neutral oil in a small saucepan on medium heat and give them the odd stir about until golden.

Meanwhile, stand a heatproof sieve with the remaining sliced shallots in the sink, then pour the boiling water over. Shake to remove residual water, then transfer into a small bowl. Add the lime juice, along with the grated palm sugar, stir about and leave to stand until the shallots turn pink. Rinse and dry the sieve.

Once the fried shallots are golden brown and crispy (about 5 minutes), strain through the sieve into a heatproof bowl (so you can reuse the oil). Transfer the fried shallots onto paper towel to further drain, and reserve for garnish.

For the eggplant glaze, heat a large heavy-based frying pan on medium heat. Rinse the eggplant to remove excess salt, then transfer to the pan along with the boiling water and crank it to high heat, tossing for 8–10 minutes to evaporate the liquid. Once the eggplant is browned on all sides, pour in the reserved shallot oil and fry for 4–5 minutes until the eggplant is glistening and golden.

2 glossy eggplants (aubergines), about 1 kg (2 lb 4 oz)

1 teaspoon salt flakes

1 cos (romaine) lettuce, leaves pulled apart and soaked in cold water

4 watermelon radishes, finely sliced and soaked in cold water

½ cup coriander (cilantro) leaves, reserving the prettiest for garnish

¼ cup Thai basil leaves, reserving the prettiest for garnish

¼ cup mint leaves

1 long red chilli, finely sliced, plus extra for serving

A LOTTA SHALLOTS

4 banana shallots (see page 17), julienned

¼ cup (60 ml) neutral oil (I like grapeseed or rice bran)

1 cup (250 ml) boiling water

Juice of 2 limes

1 tablespoon palm sugar (jaggery), grated

EGGPLANT GLAZE

½ cup (125 ml) boiling water

4 garlic cloves, grated

40 g (1½ oz) ginger, grated

2 tablespoons finely chopped
    lemongrass stem

¼ bunch coriander (cilantro) stems,
    washed well and finely chopped

4 tablespoons soy sauce

50 g (1¾ oz) palm sugar (jaggery),
    grated and dissolved in 3 tablespoons
    of just-boiled water

FINAL BITS & BOBS

1 juicy lime

Add the garlic, ginger, lemongrass and coriander stems to the pan. Sauté for 2 minutes, tossing continuously, then add the soy sauce and palm sugar water, continuing to cook until all of the liquid has been absorbed and the mix is glossy and glazed. Switch off the heat, then pour the lime juice from the bottom of the lime-quickled shallots into the glazed eggplant pan and stir about to incorporate. Taste and season with salt and pepper if necessary.

Drain and dry the lettuce leaves and arrange on a platter or serving bowl. When ready to serve, toss the eggplant (still warm or cooled – whatever floats your boat) with the radishes, herbs and chilli, then tumble onto the lettuce. Top with quickled and crispy shallots, finishing with reserved pretty leaves, extra chilli and lime cheeks or wedges.

FRIENDS WITH

Green mango, pomelo & herb būn p68

Adjapsandal is one of my fave Georgian go-tos, no matter the season. Its more traditional form is broody and stewy, designed to burble away on the winter stove like ratatouille, but with more fresh herbs. In summer, while the barbecue's on and veg like these are va-va-voom, it makes sense to just chuck 'em on the barbie instead. Team with a spicy shortcut adjika paste using a jar of roasted peppers. Piquillo are the best if you can find them, but you can use the ones from the deli counter too, with a splash more red wine vin to balance the acidity, tasting as you go. You could also do this on a griddle inside if it's not barbecue weather – make sure to get it smoking hot and open a window!

Barbecued adjapsandal *with* adjika yoghurt dressing

Preheat the barbecue or grill plate until smoking.

Pop eggplant and zucchini on one tray and onion and tomato on another. Brush the eggplant generously with olive oil (you can use an olive oil spray if you like). The zucchini doesn't need as much oil – the residual oil on the grill is plenty.

Place the eggplant on the open grill side of the barbecue for 10–15 minutes, turning halfway, until cooked through and with defined char marks (more is more with eggplant, really). Transfer the cooked eggplant slices to the upper rack to keep warm (if you don't have an upper rack, pop them back onto the tray and loosely cover with foil). Grill the zucchini for 6–8 minutes, flipping halfway.

Repeat with the tomato and onion, until they are slightly blackened and blistered and seeping out juice. As each item is cooked, introduce them to the eggplant on the upper rack (or in the loosely covered tray) to keep warm too.

Make the adjika by putting all of the ingredients into a small blender and whizzing until smooth. Taste and season with salt and pepper.

When ready to serve, blob the yoghurt and the adjika together on a large serving platter, schmearing with a flexible spatula or the back of a spoon to create a marbled pattern. Put the warm grilled vegetables on top and finish with extra olive oil, reserved coriander leaves and extra basil leaves.

1 large or 2 medium eggplants (aubergines), about 500 g (1 lb 2 oz), sliced into 1 cm (⅜ inch) discs

2 large zucchini (courgette), about 400 g (14 oz), sliced into 1 cm (⅜ inch) discs

1 large red onion, about 250 g (9 oz), sliced into 1 cm (⅜ inch) rings

4 large truss tomatoes, about 400 g (14 oz), quartered vertically

¼ cup (60 ml) extra virgin olive oil, plus extra for brushing

ADJIKA

4 garlic cloves

¼ cup (40 g) sundried tomatoes, drained

1 cup drained piquillo peppers, about 250 g (9 oz)

¼ teaspoon mild chilli flakes

15 g (½ oz) coriander (cilantro) stems, leaves reserved

15 g (½ oz) parsley stems and leaves

15 g (½ oz) holy basil, Thai basil or young regular basil leaves, plus extra for garnish

30 ml (1 fl oz) neutral oil (I like sunflower or grapeseed here)

1 teaspoon ground fenugreek

1 teaspoon ground coriander

1 teaspoon salt flakes

½ teaspoon sugar

¼ teaspoon pepper

FINAL BITS & BOBS

1 cup (230 g) natural yoghurt

FRIENDS WITH

Cauli tabouli with lemony tahini and pomegranate p62

Strawb sweetness against the pepperiness of rocket and black pepper is a combination that deserves a comeback. Strawberry behaves like tomato here – indeed, most tomato salads could have a red berry replacement. White salad onion (often sold with a green shoot springing out of its top) is nice and mild if you can find it, but red onion would be a suitable sub. You could do the parmesan lace as crackers if you're travelling with the salad – just sprinkle little mounds with a bit of space between, and keep in an airtight container (in the cupboard, not the fridge!) until go-time. To max out on sweetness, pick the most aromatic strawbs, then cap your maceration time at 15 minutes.

Strawberry & rocket salad *with* peppery parmesan

Preheat oven to 180°C (350°F) or 160°C (320°F) fan forced. Line a baking tray with baking paper.

To make the peppery parmesan lace, use the tips of your fingers to sprinkle a layer of parmesan on the prepared baking tray and crack the pepper over from a height. To collect the amount you need, crack it into your palm and measure, if you prefer to be precise. Bake for 4–5 minutes until the cheese has melted and turned into a golden parmesan sheet. Pull out of the oven and leave to cool on the tray.

Put rocket and basil leaves in a bowl or salad spinner and cover with cold water.

Pop prepared strawberries in another bowl and sprinkle with the sugar, salt flakes and a grind of pepper. Leave to macerate for 15 minutes.

To assemble the salad, drain and spin the rocket and basil leaves, then gently toss together with the macerated strawberries. Transfer onto a large platter and nestle in the bocconcini and salad onion slices.

To make the polka-dot dressing, pour the olive oil into a small bowl or saucer, then add balsamic to the bowl. Swirl the two together until a polka-dot pattern emerges. Pour dressing over the top of the salad.

Arrange the parmesan lace over the top like Eliza Doolittle's glow-up hat in *My Fair Lady*.

Serve at once.

100 g (3½ oz) baby rocket (arugula)

¼ cup loosely packed basil leaves

500 g (1 lb 2 oz) strawberries, hulled and halved

½ teaspoon caster (superfine) sugar

½ teaspoon salt flakes

PEPPERY PARMESAN LACE

50 g (1¾ oz) parmesan cheese, finely grated

¼ teaspoon coarsely cracked black pepper

POLKA-DOT DRESSING

¼ cup (60 ml) extra virgin olive oil

1 tablespoon aged balsamic vinegar

FINAL BITS & BOBS

125 g (4½ oz) drained bocconcini balls

½ salad onion, finely sliced into half-moons

FRIENDS WITH

Shaved zucchini & edamame salad with pickled ginger p76

Make this in a food processor or using one of those fancy Japanese mandolins, because you want it to be super uniform and slim: 3–4 mm (⅛ inch) will do it. If you can't find black sesame seeds, toast up some white ones. You could throw in extras if you have them, particularly spring onion slices or a handful of blanched green peas – but hold off on the carrot if you can, to keep it pale (if you want a more colourful slaw, you'll find one on page 160). This will last a couple of days, but the cabbage will keep releasing its own liquid, so give it another stir just before serving.

Japanese snow slaw *with* wasabi mayo dressing

Start by making the dressing. Combine the ingredients in a large bowl that will fit the rest of the salad.

Using a mandolin, shave the cabbage as thinly as you can, then peel and finely slice the kohlrabi into thin matchsticks using a julienne attachment. Pop them straight into the dressing as you go, along with the sliced salad onion, tossing to coat.

Leave to macerate and release more liquid for 20 minutes or so prior to serving, tossing again to incorporate the dressing, before transferring to a platter and sprinkling with black sesame seeds.

500 g (1 lb 2 oz) white cabbage, approximately ¼ of a head

1 kohlrabi, about 400 g (14 oz)

1 small white salad onion, halved and finely sliced against the grain

WASABI MAYO DRESSING

1 tablespoon mirin

¼ cup (60 g) Kewpie mayonnaise

1 teaspoon wasabi (fresh or from a tube)

½ teaspoon salt flakes

FINAL BITS & BOBS

1 tablespoon black sesame seeds

FRIENDS WITH

Honeydew carpaccio with coriander pesto p64

Snow-white wintertime
fine dark footsteps track over
the mayonnaise mound

The higher the mercury climbs, the more moisture content your salad should contain, and you can't get wetter than watermelon and cucumber. The key with adding these to salads is to hold the dressing until just before serving, because watermelon breaks down and releases liquid quicker than a debutante with a dodgy hem. The dressing in question is also terrifically low-waste, utilising the brine and whey of your bits and bobs; if you want to zero in even further, try pickling the watermelon rind, or peel off the green outer skin, slice finely and stir-fry as you would broccoli stalks.

Watermelon salad *with* chilli feta dressing

½ cup (70 g) kalamata olives

2 Lebanese cucumbers

¼ seedless watermelon, peeled and coarsely chopped

½ red onion, thinly sliced into rounds

¼ cup small mint leaves, loosely packed

150 g (5½ oz) Greek feta, drained and whey reserved

CHILLI FETA DRESSING

2 tablespoons feta whey

1 long red chilli, finely sliced

1 garlic clove, bruised

¼ cup (60 ml) extra virgin olive oil

2 tablespoons lemon juice

Combine the dressing ingredients in a jar, shaking to emulsify, then set aside until just before serving.

If olives are still with-pit, squash under the base of your olive oil bottle, or between thumb and forefinger to remove the pits, or use an olive pitter.

Use a julienne peeler or scrape the tines of a fork down the sides of the peeled cucumbers to help create ridges that soak up more dressing, then chop into jaunty chunks.

Combine cucumber, watermelon, onion, olives and mint in a shallow salad bowl or on a serving platter, then crumble feta over. Fish the bruised garlic clove out of the dressing, then drizzle dressing over the top of the salad, sprinkling with a scant pinch of salt flakes and cracked pepper. Toss again at the table.

FRIENDS WITH
Salat olivye p90

As far as stone fruit, adjectives and emojis go, peaches promise playfulness and satisfaction. Even the hardest, hapless peach is not irredeemable. Lacklustre peaches can be dialled up with time on the barbecue, their natural zip and sweetness caramelising to something entirely more sophisticated (plums and nectarines are also happy grillers). If your peaches are already super sweet, don't even bother grilling – just slice into wedges and serve with the rest of the stuff. If you've snapped up green peppercorns for this, use the rest to make a sauce for roast veg or steak. Pink peppercorns fit the bill if you can't find green – just halve the quantity and grind in a mortar and pestle. Buffalo mozza is a worthy stand-in for burrata.

Grilled peach salad *with* burrata *and* green peppercorns

Heat a barbecue grill plate or heavy-based griddle pan on medium heat. Have a piece of baking paper and foil handy (this'll help keep the peaches intact, without leaving half the best burnished bits on the grill).

Cut peaches in half and remove the stone.

Brush the cut peach halves with a little of the olive oil. Lay the baking paper on top of the foil, then lay it foil-side down onto the hot grill, placing the peaches cut-side down on top of the baking paper.

Cook for 5–10 minutes until the peaches have burnished evenly, softening slightly, then turn over to just warm through.

Meanwhile, to make the vinaigrette, put all of the ingredients into a small bowl and whisk until emulsified. Taste and season with salt and pepper.

Place the peaches cut-side up on a serving platter, leaving gaps for the burrata balls. Remove the garlic clove from the vinaigrette and pour the dressing over the peaches while they are still hot. Blob in the burrata, scatter with the mint leaves and finely sliced chives and dress with salt and pepper and a final flourish of olive oil.

6–8 firm ripe freestone peaches

1 tablespoon extra virgin olive oil, plus extra for finishing

GREEN PEPPERCORN VINAIGRETTE

1 bruised garlic clove

1 teaspoon green peppercorns, chopped

2 teaspoons white wine vinegar

1 teaspoon honey

1 teaspoon dijon mustard

¼ teaspoon salt flakes

FINAL BITS & BOBS

2–3 burrata balls, about 120 g (4¼ oz) each, drained

¼ cup loosely packed mint leaves

2 tablespoons finely sliced chives

FRIENDS WITH

Mimosa lettuce with retro dressing p100

If grainy salads have been off the table at your place, rejoice! This is an easy recipe to make GF by subbing in more cauli – some pulsed to rice and some kept finely sliced. If grains are a goer, then find some freekeh, which is lovely and nutty. You could of course go tradish with burghul (if you've got any left from the Cypriot salad on page 156), or use up the box of couscous sitting in your cupboard. There are some nifty ways to deseed pomegranate (for tips, see page 156). This salad will last 2–3 days in the fridge.

Cauli tabouli *with* lemony tahini *and* pomegranate

Bring 1½ cups (375 ml) well-salted water to the boil in a medium saucepan. Rinse the freekeh and scoop into the pot along with the reserved mint stems. Bring the water back to boil, cover, then drop to simmer on a very low heat for 20–25 minutes, until the liquid evaporates and the freekeh is tender to the squeeze.

Meanwhile, put the tomato and cucumber in a bowl and mix with the salt and sugar. Set aside to rest for at least 10 minutes to extract excess juice. Once this is done, drain and reserve the juice.

Fish the mint stems out of the freekeh. Pour the reserved cucumber and tomato juice over the freekeh and fluff with a fork, as you would couscous.

Place the cauli cut-side down on the chopping board and use a sharp knife to finely shave, following its shape.

Collect the cauli and herbs in a large mixing bowl, along with the drained tomato and cucumber, spring onions, red onion, toasted almonds (keeping some for garnish) and half of the pomegranate seeds. Plonk in the freekeh, including any residual juices from the bottom of the pot.

To make the lemon and tahini dressing, put the lemon zest and juice into a small bowl with the tahini, garlic, salt and pepper and whisk well. Whisk in the olive oil, taste and season with more salt and pepper if needed.

Pour the dressing into the large mixing bowl with the veg and fold everything together until glossy. Taste again and adjust the seasoning, especially noticing if it needs more salt or acid (a lemon cheek or two to serve should set that straight). Set aside for 15 minutes to get friendly before serving, then give everything another stir and transfer onto a serving platter, finishing with remaining pomegranate seeds and almond slivers.

½ cup (90 g) cracked freekeh

½ bunch mint, leaves picked and finely chopped, stems reserved

1 large ripe tomato, diced

2 Lebanese cucumbers, diced

1 teaspoon salt flakes

¼ teaspoon caster (superfine) sugar

½ cauliflower, washed well

½ bunch curly parsley, ends trimmed

2 spring onions (scallions), finely sliced

½ red onion, finely diced

½ cup (65 g) slivered almonds, toasted

Seeds of 1 pomegranate

LEMONY TAHINI DRESSING

Zest and juice of 1 lemon

2 tablespoons tahini

1–2 garlic cloves, minced

1 teaspoon salt flakes

¼ teaspoon freshly cracked pepper

½ cup (125 ml) extra virgin olive oil

FINAL BITS & BOBS

Lemon cheeks (optional)

FRIENDS WITH

Barbecued adjapsandal with adjika yoghurt dressing p52

This is a very adaptable recipe for any firm fruit in your fridge or fruit bowl: melons, stone fruit – heck, even pineapple! The key is to use a sharp knife and slice against the grain for the best mouthfeel, as you might sashimi. Some people don't like coriander (they're wrong) but you could use basil to make your pesto instead. The pesto could easily be made days in advance and loosened off with extra oil if need be. Serve chilled on a hot summer's day for a refreshing(ly!) easy talking point.

Honeydew carpaccio *with* coriander pesto

To make the coriander pesto, muddle the ingredients in a mortar and pestle or put them into a food processor and blitz until smooth. Taste and season with more salt and pepper if necessary. Set aside in a clean jar if making ahead, or in a bowl if ready to serve.

Toss the cherry tomato and baby cucumber rounds in the lime juice.

Place honeydew slices on a platter and scatter with the juicy cherry tomato and baby cucumber rounds. Drizzle with the coriander pesto and sprinkle with sliced chilli, chopped peanuts and reserved coriander sprigs. Serve with lime cheeks.

1 perfectly ripe honeydew melon, about 1.2 kg (2 lb 12 oz), peeled and sliced thinly into half-moons

1 punnet yellow cherry tomatoes (or lightbulb tomatoes), about 200 g (7 oz), thinly sliced

1 punnet baby cucumbers, about 250 g (9 oz), thinly sliced into rounds

1 tablespoon lime juice (about half a lime's worth)

CORIANDER PESTO

¼ bunch coriander (cilantro), pretty sprigs reserved for garnish

¼ cup (40 g) salted roasted peanuts

1 cup baby spinach leaves, refreshed in chilled water

½ cup (125 ml) neutral oil (I like peanut or rice bran here)

1 garlic clove

½ tablespoon fish sauce

½ tablespoon sesame oil

Zest and juice of 1 lime

½ teaspoon sugar

½ teaspoon salt

1 pinch freshly cracked black pepper

FINAL BITS & BOBS

1 long green chilli, finely sliced

¼ cup (40 g) salted roasted peanuts, chopped

Lime cheeks

FRIENDS WITH

Japanese snow slaw with wasabi mayo dressing p56

Look, I know you're probably thinking, 'What's there to learn about fruit salad?' Well, if you want a Grown Up fruit salad, there are some points to note. You want each bite to contain variety, which means considering colour, texture (firmer or softer), and varying the cuts to highlight each natural shape. You also don't want the salad to hit one note flavour-wise, which is where the salty crumb comes in as a lovely counterpoint. If lychees are in season, use freshies, but the tinned ones come complete with syrup that is just begging to be repurposed into a margarita.

Fruit salad *with* zesty dressing *and* salty–sweet macadamias

565 g (20 oz) tin lychees in syrup, drained and halved, syrup reserved for the dressing

1 small pineapple, about 900 g (2 lb), peeled and sliced

½ ripe red papaya, about 500 g (1 lb 2 oz), peeled and sliced

1 firm ripe mango, about 400 g (14 oz), peeled and cubed

¼ cup (60 ml) passionfruit pulp (1 juicy fruit's worth)

THAI BASIL DRESSING

3–4 Thai basil stems, leaves picked and reserved

1 thumb ginger, grated

Zest and juice of 1 lime, plus extra juice if needed

SALTED MACADAMIA CRUMB

½ cup (35 g) shredded coconut

½ cup (75 g) raw macadamia nuts, roughly chopped

½ teaspoon icing sugar

¼ teaspoon salt flakes

To make the macadamia crumb, put the coconut and chopped macadamias in a frying pan over low heat and shake the pan until the coconut turns golden, then turn off the heat. Toss with the icing sugar and salt flakes and set aside to cool. Once cooled, this can be stored in an airtight jar until ready to serve.

To make the dressing, pour ¼ cup (60 ml) of the reserved lychee syrup into the bottom of a large mixing bowl. Whack the Thai basil stems with the back of your knife and pop these in the bowl to steep for 10 minutes or so. Squeeze the grated ginger in your fist to extract the juice into the bowl, discarding the fuzz, and add the lime zest and juice.

Remove the basil stems from the bowl and discard. Add the fruit to the mixing bowl and gently fold through the dressing, tasting and adding extra lime to balance the sweetness if need be. Set aside to macerate for up to 15 minutes before serving.

Just before serving, add the basil leaves to the mixing bowl and toss about. Tumble into a serving bowl and finish with macadamia crumb sprinkled from a height.

BONUS RECIPE
SERVES 4

100 ml (3½ fl oz) lime juice (4 limes should do it), plus extra wedges to garnish

Salt flakes, for rimming your glasses

100 ml (3½ fl oz) lychee syrup, plus 4 lychees to garnish (optional)

200 ml (7 fl oz) tequila

Ice cubes, to serve

Lychee margarita

Put 1 tablespoon of the lime juice in a saucer and salt flakes in another saucer. Dip the rims of the 4 glasses into the lime juice, then dip in the salt flakes.

In a jug, mix the rest of the lime juice with the lychee syrup and tequila.

Fill the rimmed tumblers with ice. Pour the lychee margarita mix into the glasses, then pop a wedge of lime on the side of each one to garnish.

This is somewhere between a substantial salad and a chilled summer soup, so even though it looks like you're making a lot of dressing, you really want to drown your noodles in it. You can use vermicelli rice noodles as is traditional here, or go for a twist with mung bean noodles (particularly if you have some left over from making the Rock 'n' roll salad on page 114). I've kept this vego, with coconut as the fleshy component – you could even make it vegan by subbing out the fish sauce – but you could also go the whole prawn by adding cooked ones and/or some dried shrimp too. If you can't find young coconut, or can't be bothered fussing with it, use 1 cup (250 ml) of coconut water instead.

Green mango, pomelo & herb būn

To make the dressing, use a cleaver or heavy knife to whack the top of the coconut to create a lid. Pour the coconut water through a sieve into a large mixing bowl – you'll need about 250 ml (1 cup) of liquid. Scoop out the flesh with a spoon and finely slice, then set aside.

Squeeze the ginger in a tight fist to extract all of the juice into the bowl, discarding the fuzz. Add the rest of the dressing ingredients. Taste for balance – some limes and coconut waters are sweeter than others. If you need to, add more palm sugar or fish sauce.

Use a julienne peeler to slice the green mango. Alternatively, use a sharp knife to cut thin sheets of mango flesh and slice into matchsticks. Toss the mango and noodles in the dressing, to get friendly.

Add coconut flesh, lettuce, pomelo and banana shallot to the mixing bowl, and toss about to coat in the dressing too.

Transfer to a large serving bowl, and top with herbs, peanuts and lime cheeks.

1 firm mango (green or just underripe)

50 g (1¾ oz) rice vermicelli noodles, cooked to packet instructions

½ small iceberg lettuce, shredded

1 pomelo, peeled and segmented

1 banana shallot (see page 17), julienned

FRESH COCONUT WATER DRESSING

1 fresh young coconut (water and flesh)

1 thumb ginger, grated

2–3 garlic cloves, minced

Zest and juice of 2 limes

¼ cup (60 ml) funky fish sauce, plus extra if needed

2 tablespoons (40 g) palm sugar (jaggery), grated, plus extra if needed

2–3 birdseye chillies, finely sliced

1 lemongrass stem, thinly sliced diagonally against the grain

FINAL BITS & BOBS

Handful Vietnamese mint leaves

Handful Thai basil leaves

Handful mint sprigs (optional but excellent)

2 tablespoons chopped roasted peanuts

2 limes, sliced into cheeks

FRIENDS WITH

Eggplant larb with fresh, quickled & fried shallots p48

Moghrabieh is a lot like fregola, palm-rolled pearl-shaped couscous made from durum wheat. Are you making a pasta salad by another name? Why yes, yes you are. Use the hand-rolled moghrabieh rather than the machine-pressed. It's got a bigger pearl, and gives you better bite when cooked. Depending on the type you've got, cooking time will vary so, as with all pasta, don't follow me, follow the back of the packet! If you've got spring onions (scallions) in the fridge or garden, they're a welcome addition here, but don't head out to the shops for them. Neither should you be making a special trip for ras el hanout: check online recipes to see if you already have the makings from the spices at your disposal.

Green veg moghrabieh *with* yoghurt drizzle

Boil a large saucepan of well-salted water. Cook moghrabieh for 18–20 minutes (timing may vary, so check the packet instructions to be sure) at a gentle boil until tender.

While the moghrabieh is cooking, cut the broccolini stems into pea-sized cubes, then use a cross-chop to make the florets pea-sized too.

Pop the slivered almonds in a frying pan and toss over medium heat until lightly golden. Remove the almonds from the pan and set aside, then keep heating the pan until very hot.

Toss the haloumi cubes in a teaspoon or so of the olive oil, then place on the hot pan and cook on all sides until golden.

Prep a high-sided, wide tray with 2 tablespoons of olive oil and spread the cubed zucchini and teeny broccolini florets in its base. Check the moghrabieh at the 18 minute mark, as you would pasta. If it's fully tender at this point, scoop it out and shake it flat onto the tray. If it still has some chalkiness through the centre, keep it in the pot. Pop the frozen peas and broccolini stem cubes into the boiling water for 2 minutes.

Drain the moghrabieh and veg through a heatproof sieve, then tip it all straight onto the tray with the zucchini and broccolini florets, shaking about to get friendly. Set aside to cool.

1 heaped cup large moghrabieh (pearl couscous), about 180 g (6¼ oz)

2 bunches broccolini, about 400 g (14 oz)

½ cup (65 g) slivered almonds

200 g (7 oz) haloumi, patted very dry and cut into cubes

¼ cup (60 ml) extra virgin olive oil, plus extra for finishing

1 medium to large zucchini (courgette), about 150 g (5½ oz), cubed

1 cup (140 g) frozen peas

RAS EL HANOUT YOGHURT DRIZZLE

½ cup (125 ml) extra virgin olive oil

1–2 garlic cloves

½ bunch mint, stems coarsely chopped, leaves picked, ¼ reserved for garnish

½ bunch coriander (cilantro), stems coarsely chopped, leaves picked, ¼ reserved for garnish

Zest and juice of 1 lemon

1½ teaspoons salt flakes

¼ teaspoon freshly ground pepper

½ cup (130 g) natural yoghurt

¼ cup (65 g) tahini

2 teaspoons runny honey

1½ teaspoons ground ras el hanout

FINAL BITS & BOBS

2 spring onions (scallions), very finely sliced

FRIENDS WITH

Baked cauli & feta salad with golden raisin dressing p146

Make the ras el hanout yoghurt drizzle in a food processor by pouring in the olive oil, garlic, mint and coriander stems and leaves, lemon zest and juice, salt and pepper. Whizz to mince the garlic and break up the stalks to a fine green paste. Pour in the yoghurt and tahini, along with the honey and ras el hanout, and blitz again until totally smooth. Taste and season with more salt and pepper if needed.

Plonk the haloumi in with the moghrabieh and veg and toss about to get super glossy in the oil. Transfer to a platter, then drizzle the dressing over and top with the slivered almonds, reserved mint and coriander leaves and the spring onions. Serve with an extra drizzle of extra virgin olive oil.

HAND-ROLLED

MACHINE-PRESSED

You've probably noticed by now that I love burning veg, and it's the types you least expect to find forged in fire that taste the most enticing. If your baby zucchini come with flowers as a gift-with-purchase, tear the petals through this salad for extra texture and colour. Considering the Middle Eastern leanings of this flavour profile, *urfa* or Aleppo pepper flakes are best for the chilli oil, but any ol' mild one will do you too. Labneh is super set-and-forget – literally, but it does need to be started a day ahead, so do yourself a favour and make a double batch, then you've got enough for the salad AND to roll bonus labneh balls.

Charred & smashed zucchini *with* labneh *and* chilli oil

250 g (9 oz) baby zucchini (courgette), flowers welcome and encouraged

6 small to medium mixed green and yellow zucchini, about 800 g (1 lb 12 oz)

LABNEH

1 teaspoon salt flakes

500 g (1 lb 2 oz) full-fat natural yoghurt

ZA'ATAR CHILLI OIL DRIZZLE

½ cup (125 ml) extra virgin olive oil

1 teaspoon mild chilli flakes

1–2 garlic cloves, minced

2 tablespoons za'atar

Zest and juice of 1 lemon

½ teaspoon salt flakes

FINAL BITS & BOBS

1 tablespoon toasted sesame seeds

2 tablespoons mint leaves

2 tablespoons basil leaves

To make the labneh, stir salt into the yoghurt then hang in muslin (cheesecloth) overnight over a bowl in the fridge.

Finely slice the baby zucchini into discs, reserving any accompanying flowers for garnish. Blacken the larger zucchini undressed over a low and slow open flame (or on a barbecue grill plate) on all sides as you would an eggplant for baba ganoush, for 15–20 minutes until soft to the touch.

Meanwhile, to make the za'atar chilli oil drizzle, heat the oil to shimmering. Put chilli flakes, garlic and za'atar in a heatproof bowl and carefully pour the oil over the top. Stir in the lemon zest and juice, wait for it to cool a little, then taste and season with salt and pepper.

Toss the baby zucchini into the oil to get friendly.

Smash charred zucchini a little with the flat of a tablespoon until the creamy innards show.

Smooth labneh on the serving plate. Arrange the charred and smashed zucchini over the top, then drizzle the za'atar chilli oil over, finishing with torn zucchini flowers (if using), toasted sesame seeds, mint, basil. Season with salt and pepper to serve.

BONUS RECIPE
SERVES 4–6

Marinated labneh balls

500 g (1 lb 2 oz) full-fat natural yoghurt

1 teaspoon salt flakes

2 tablespoons finely chopped parsley leaves

2 tablespoons za'atar

2 tablespoon toasted sesame seeds

Extra virgin olive oil, for preserving

Combine yoghurt with salt flakes, then hang overnight in muslin (cheesecloth) over a bowl in the fridge.

Toss together the parsley, za'atar and sesame seeds in a bowl. Scoop heaped teaspoons of labneh straight into the bowl, tossing about to coat, then shaping into balls with your hands.

Pour oil halfway up a sterilised jar, then drop the balls in, topping up with oil to cover if need be. Alternatively, serve labneh balls fresh on top of leafy salad or under a juicy sliced tomato on toast.

This is a dump 'n' dress salad, so there's no need to emulsify the dressing ahead of time. The raw zucchini cures in the sharp, warming dressing, but it's still a surprisingly robust salad which will last a few days in the fridge – though it's at its optimal point texturally at around the 1–2 hour mark, while the zucchini still has some bite. Pickled ginger can be a little bitter so do taste for balance and add a small amount of extra sugar if needed. You could add a soba noodle here to make it a more substantial meal-in-a-bowl. Mukimame are the podded version of edamame, and you should be able to find them in the freezer aisle. If you can't, buy whole edamame and pod them after blanching.

Shaved zucchini & edamame salad *with* pickled ginger

Bring a medium saucepan of well-salted water to the boil, then tumble in the mukimame and cook for 2 minutes. Drain and set aside.

Peel long strips of zucchini on the diagonal, using a julienne mandolin or peeler.

Put the zucchini, mukimame and the coriander into a bowl and add the dressing ingredients straight on top, giving everything a bit of a mix, then set aside until ready to serve.

Arrange the mixture on a platter, drizzling with any leftover dressing from the bottom of the bowl, and dressing with some extra olive oil. Season with salt and pepper.

Serve straight away, or leave to soften and get friendly. Sprinkle with crushed wasabi peas just before it hits the table.

1 cup (150 g) frozen mukimame (podded edamame) beans

4 small to medium zucchini (courgette), about 600 g (1 lb 5 oz)

½ cup roughly chopped coriander (cilantro) leaves and stems

PICKLED GINGER DRESSING

1 tablespoon pickled ginger, finely chopped

1 tablespoon pickled ginger juice

2 spring onions (scallions), finely sliced

1 tablespoon mirin

1 tablespoon lemon juice

1 tablespoon sesame oil

2 tablespoons extra virgin olive oil, plus extra for drizzling

1½ teaspoons salt flakes

FINAL BITS & BOBS

1 tablespoon wasabi peas, lightly crushed in a mortar and pestle

FRIENDS WITH

Strawberry & rocket salad with peppery parmesan p54

You haven't lived til you've corkscrewed a cucumber! It does take a hot minute to get your head and hands around it, though, so you could easily just whack at them instead if you're not in the mood to get technical. Gochujang is a Korean chilli paste that is full of funk and rising heat. If you've bought some gochujang especially to make this, why not give the wombok quick-chi (see page 141) a whirl with some of the leftovers? If you can't find shiso, feel free to use more fresh coriander instead, but the broody plum tone of shiso leaf is very spesh, so if you're already at the shops buying gochujang, check whether they've got some shiso in the herb section too.

Cucumber corkscrews *with* gochujang dressing

Place each cucumber between 2 chopsticks, slice one side on a 45 degree angle every 5 mm (¼ inch). Flip over and cut straight across, matching up the ends of the diagonal cuts. Sprinkle with salt flakes and toss about to coat. Set these aside to cure, then strain off the liquid after 10 minutes.

To make the dressing, whisk together the gochujang paste, mirin, soy sauce, sesame oil and grated ginger in a large bowl.

Chuck the cucumber spirals into the bowl with the dressing and gently toss about to coat.

Transfer the spirals and dressing onto a serving platter and toss with spring onion, chilli and herbs. Scatter with toasted sesame seeds and crispy shallots.

8 Lebanese cucumbers, about 800 g (1 lb 12 oz)

1 teaspoon salt flakes

3 spring onions (scallions), thinly sliced

1 long green chilli, thinly sliced

1 punnet red shiso microherb leaves (or shiso leaves if you can't get micros)

SPICY GOCHUJANG DRESSING

2 tablespoons gochujang paste

2 tablespoons mirin

1 tablespoon soy sauce

1 tablespoon sesame oil

1 tablespoon finely grated ginger

FINAL BITS & BOBS

2 tablespoons toasted sesame seeds

2 tablespoons fried shallots

FRIENDS WITH

Wombok quick-chi salad p141

This salad was, is and always will be a staple at our place for breakfast. Growing up, no matter where we travelled in the world, Mum and Dad would pop to the local shops and buy these ingredients, fishing out their trusty camping knife and travel chopping board to kickstart our day. There's no need to get finicky with the chopping – wherever you're at on the cutting continuum is good enough. This is a base: you could add more to it, such as a firm avocado, some kind of green leaf (cos or rocket) or any soft herb. You can even keep leftovers and add to them the next day. If you want to you can easily add stale bread to soak up the tomato gloop and turn it into a panzanella, or add pita for fattoush.

Relaxed chopped salad

To make the dressing, combine the lemon juice, salt and pepper in a large mixing bowl, stirring about to help dissolve the salt a little. Pour in the olive oil and stir this about too.

Chuck in all of the chopped veggies and toss to coat. Give the mixture a taste, just in case you need to add any more salt and pepper for balance.

If serving to guests, transfer to your nice bowl. If serving for breakfast to fam, keep it in the mixing bowl. Sprinkle the herbs over the top, letting the colours mingle and dance.

2 Lebanese cucumbers, about 260 g (9¼ oz), zebra peeled (in stripes) and roughly chopped

4 ripe, aromatic tomatoes, about 500 g (1 lb 2 oz), roughly chopped

1 red capsicum (pepper), chopped into 2 cm (¾ inch) jaunty pieces

1 yellow capsicum (pepper), chopped into 2 cm (¾ inch) jaunty pieces

½ red onion, chopped into 1 cm (⅜ inch) pieces

SIMPLE SALAD DRESSING

Juice of 1 lemon (about ¼ cup/60 ml)

½ teaspoon salt flakes

¼ teaspoon freshly cracked pepper

¼ cup (60 ml) extra virgin olive oil

FINAL BITS & BOBS

½ cup finely chopped parsley leaves

¼ cup finely chopped dill leaves

¼ cup finely chopped coriander (cilantro) leaves

FRIENDS WITH
Everything!

One interpretation of the name of this Indonesian hero salad is 'hodgepodge', which should tell you all you need to know if you look down the list of ingredients and worry you're missing a few. This salad is muscling to be the main event at your next summer party. The sweet potato and marinated tempeh are meaty, and the sauce is salty–sweet and satisfying. Its creaminess does hinge on the coconut milk, so seek one in a Tetrapak, as I find these more reliably rich and emulsified. This is a recipe where it pays to have some iced water handy for refreshing everything, because it's all about the crunch factor and the contrast of crispy, cold veg against velvety satay sauce.

Gado gado platter *with* pantry satay sauce

Heat a heavy-based chargrill pan or barbecue to smoking hot. Toss the sweet potato in a tablespoon of oil, then pop the slices on and leave for 5–6 minutes on each side until the char marks are quite defined. You'll know the sweet potato is ready to flip when it starts to bead and sweat on top. Once the sweet potato comes off the grill, do the same with the tempeh (or if it fits, nestle the tempeh in with the sweet potato, too).

Meanwhile, bring a medium saucepan of well-salted water to the boil. Top the beans and slice into thirds, then cook for 3 minutes. Scoop out into cold water (ideally with ice included), keeping the boiling water on the stove. Gently place the eggs in the water, then drop to a simmer and set a timer for 6 minutes. Once the eggs have cooked, scoop the beans out of the water bowl onto paper towel to drain and dry, and pop the eggs into the bowl of water to stop the cooking and make them easier to peel. When the eggs are cool to the touch, peel and slice into quarters.

1 sweet potato, about 400 g (14 oz), sliced into 1 cm (⅜ inch) discs on the bias

1 tablespoon neutral oil (I like peanut here)

200 g (7 oz) marinated tempeh, sliced into 5 mm (¼ inch) strips

200 g (7 oz) green beans

4 eggs

¼ wombok (Chinese cabbage), very finely sliced

250 g (9 oz) baby cucumbers, quartered vertically

3 large tomatoes, quartered (heirloom shapes welcome and encouraged)

100 g (3½ oz) mixed sprouts combo, washed

¼ bunch coriander (cilantro), trimmed and washed

1 banana shallot (see page 17), sliced finely with the grain

PANTRY SATAY SAUCE

¾ cup (215 g) crunchy peanut butter

400 ml (14 fl oz) creamy coconut milk

4 makrut lime leaves

1 lemongrass stem, whacked and tied
   in a bow

1 teaspoon red curry paste

1 tablespoon kecap manis (sweet
   soy sauce)

1 tablespoon fish sauce

1 garlic clove, crushed

Juice of 1 lime

FINAL BITS & BOBS

50 g fried shallots

3 makrut lime leaves, very finely sliced

2 limes, sliced into cheeks

1 long red chilli, finely sliced

2 tablespoons roasted peanuts

FRIENDS WITH

Cucumber & daikon sheets with
tahini—miso dressing p119

To make the pantry satay sauce, put all of the ingredients except for the lime juice into a small saucepan and heat gently, stirring occasionally. Bring to the boil, then simmer for 5 minutes and remove from the heat. Stir in the lime juice and taste for balance; adjust seasoning if necessary. Set aside until ready to use.

On a large platter or in a shallow bowl, arrange all of the components separately like a colour wheel around a dipping bowl of the satay sauce, and everyone can choose their own adventure, or drizzle the dressing over the veg and toss about to combine in the dressing before serving. Top with fried shallots, makrut lime leaves, lime cheeks and sliced chilli. Roughly chop the roasted peanuts and sprinkle over the sauce.

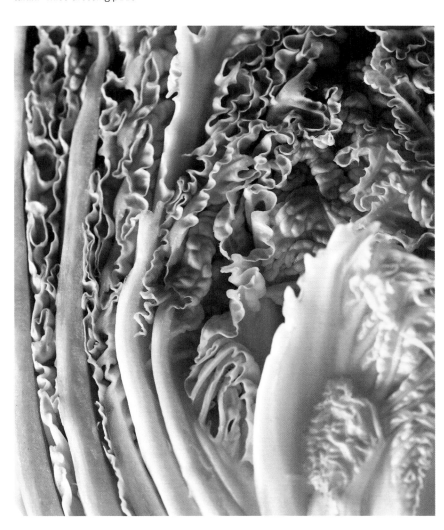

Come springtime, a version of this makes its way to our table weekly. At that point in the season, when fresh peas and broad beans are bountiful, set aside some time to pod them yourself, or buy some prepodded. Equally, you could make this later in the season, towards cooler days, using frozen peas and broadies too. Smaller broadies early in the season don't need double podding, otherwise, do put the time in for the second pod, lest you serve up blister skin (yuck, sorry). The parmesan vinaigrette is very versatile as well. Give it a drizz over bitter leaves such as radicchio, or keep it as a little dipper for lightly steamed crudités.

Easy peasy spring salad
with parmesan vinaigrette

Fork together vinaigrette ingredients until combined. Season with salt and pepper.

Bring a medium saucepan of water to the boil and tumble the podded broad beans in, then bring back to the boil for 2–4 minutes, depending on their size, until no longer chalky through the middle. Scoop out into a bowl and reserve.

Drop the peas into the boiling water and cook for 4 minutes – whether they're fresh or frozen.

Pop the snow peas and sugar snaps into a heatproof colander in the sink and pour the boiled water and peas over the top for an easy blanch.

Once the broad beans are cool enough to handle, squeeze the flesh out of the skins by finding the crack and pushing towards it. Set aside.

Give the vinaigrette a quick zhuzh to reincorporate and toss the greens through, then combine with the salad onion, snow pea sprouts, watercress, mint and parsley leaves just before serving, warm or at room temperature. Grate a final puff of parmesan over and finish with cracked pepper.

200 g (7 oz) broad beans (fava beans), podded

100 g (3½ oz) peas (frozen or fresh)

100 g (3½ oz) snow peas (mangetout), topped

100 g (3½ oz) sugar snap peas, topped

½ salad onion, finely sliced with the grain

100 g (3½ oz) snow pea sprouts

1 bunch watercress, about 100 g (3½ oz), ends trimmed

¼ cup mint leaves, finely sliced

¼ cup parsley leaves, finely sliced

PARMESAN VINAIGRETTE

2 tablespoons white wine vinegar

1–2 garlic cloves, minced

1 teaspoon dijon mustard

¼ cup (60 ml) extra virgin olive oil

25 g (1 oz) parmesan cheese, finely grated

FINAL BITS & BOBS

10 g (⅜ oz) parmesan cheese, for puffing

FRIENDS WITH

Strawberry & rocket salad with peppery parmesan p54, Japanese snow slaw with wasabi mayo dressing p56

This classic creamy potato salad is a staple of the feast table for *Novy God* (Russian New Year), and it's a great way of using up what's left of Christmas lunch. Indeed, its popularity in households throughout the Soviet Union was down to the versatility of its ingredients: stuff in tins, leftover meat or seafood, boiled carrots and potatoes ... all bound together with gloriously gloopy mayonnaise. More like Salat Oh-liv-Yeah! (Which is how you pronounce it, might I add.) I've made this one with picked crab meat (which you can buy ready-picked) but you could equally use any protein at your disposal, from Christmas ham to last night's roast chicken to a tin of big white beans.

Salat olivye

Put the potatoes, carrots and eggs into a large saucepan of well-salted water and bring to the boil. Drop it down to a simmer and pull the eggs out at the 10 minute mark. Medium carrots will take around 15 minutes while spuds are more like 20–25 minutes. Pop eggs into a bowl of chilled water (or run them under the tap), then peel and dice.

Once you scoop the potatoes and carrots out, use the pot of boiled water to cook the frozen peas for 3 minutes.

Meanwhile, make the dressing by forking together the mayonnaise with the olive oil, dill, salt and pepper, tasting for balance. Set aside.

Allow the spuds to cool enough to touch, then peel them with your hands. Rub the skin off the carrot with paper towel. Cube both potatoes and carrots with a nice sharp knife or Alligator slicer.

Combine everything together, adding dressing a couple of heaped tablespoons at a time until you're happy with the level of creaminess. This'll keep in the fridge for 2–3 days.

Transfer to a serving platter and finish with the reserved dill fronds. Set off some fireworks and give someone a peck when the clock strikes twelve. *S Novim Godom* (Happy new year)!

3 waxy potatoes, about 500 g (1 lb 2 oz), washed and scrubbed

2 carrots, about 250 g (9 oz)

6 eggs

350 g (12 oz) frozen peas

140 g (5 oz) picked crab meat

4 sour dill pickles, cubed

1 small red onion

DILL MAYO DRESSING

¾ cup (185 g) whole egg mayo

¼ cup (60 ml) extra virgin olive oil

½ bunch dill, finely chopped, reserving some fronds for garnish

½ teaspoon salt flakes

⅛ teaspoon ground white pepper

FRIENDS WITH

Watermelon salad with chilli feta dressing p59

If you're looking for a delicate salad that takes full advantage of a short local asparagus season, this is it. It's also an example of the pink-and-green-must-always-be-seen rule for great salad-ing. If your asparagus is a little wilty, trim the ends and then stand it spears-up in a jar of water as you would flowers, and it'll spring to attention again. This salad will work with a different kind of shallot – it's just that red is perfect for a really deep pink hue. Chervil doesn't get enough of a go Down Under, even though it's got such a marvellously mellow anise flavour, like mild tarragon with a hint of parsley. If you can't find it, feel free to use picked tarragon leaves or flat-leaf parsley instead.

Asparagus ribbons
with pickled pink dressing

Use a speed peeler or mandolin to run along the length of the asparagus spears, creating thin ribbons. Drop into a bowl of cold water until ready to serve.

To make the pickled pink dressing, sprinkle sugar on top of the shallot slices, then pour the vinegar and lemon juice over, stirring about until it starts to change colour. After 5 minutes, scoop out the quickled shallot and reserve, then fork in the olive oil and season with salt and pepper.

Drain and spin the asparagus to dry, then toss with the shallot and dress with the pickled pink dressing. Top with chervil sprigs and season to taste with more salt and pepper.

1 bunch thick asparagus spears, about 450 g (1 lb)

PICKLED PINK DRESSING

½ teaspoon sugar

1 red shallot (see page 17), finely sliced into rings

2 teaspoons white wine vinegar

Juice of half a lemon, plus extra for squeezing over

1 tablespoon extra virgin olive oil

FINAL BITS & BOBS

½ cup loosely packed chervil, picked into sprigs

FRIENDS WITH
Gurkensalat 2.0 p95

You might have seen this classic combination of flavours before, but has the sight of it taken your breath away? That's the power of a sharp knife and a graphic salad. You can eke a lot of wow-factor from very simple ingredients, through precision cutting, by going slow with the aforementioned sharp knife, or leaning on the odd gadget. You could deploy the mandolin to slice the cucumber and onion for uniformity instead – use a guard or eat the ends as chef snacks. If you're just making this at home, feel free to ease off on the artistry and simply slice the cucumber, adding lemon in the form of extra juice in the dressing if you wish to max out on zing. Meyer lemons would be marvellous here.

Gurkensalat 2.0

¼ cup (40 g) currants

2 telegraph cucumbers, peeled and finely sliced

¼ red onion, sliced into fine rings

¼ teaspoon each of salt flakes and caster (superfine) sugar

HERBY YOGHURT DRESSING

½ cup (130 g) natural yoghurt

Juice of half a lemon

1 garlic clove, minced

¼ cup finely chopped parsley leaves

1 tablespoon chopped coriander (cilantro) leaves

1 tablespoon finely chopped dill, picking and saving some of the prettier fronds for garnish

FINAL BITS & BOBS

1 small lemon (or half a medium one)

2 tablespoons extra virgin olive oil

In a small heatproof bowl, cover the currants with just-boiled water and set aside to plump up.

Put the cucumber slices and onion rings in a medium bowl and sprinkle with a pinch of salt and sugar, tossing about to coat, and set aside to cure for 5–10 minutes.

Make the dressing by whisking the yoghurt, lemon juice, garlic and herbs together. Taste and season with salt and pepper.

Pinwheel the lemon by first lopping off the top and bottom to stabilise, then slicing off the skin and pith. Saw away at the last of the pith, sticking as close as possible to where it meets the flesh. Once the yellow flesh is exposed on all sides, slice against the grain to create 2 mm ($\frac{1}{16}$ inch) thin discs of citrus.

Tessellate the cucumber and larger onion rings across a platter in a graphic fashion (unleash your inner Modernist), then just before serving, drizzle generously with the dressing and dot with the lemon pinwheels, drained currants and dill fronds. Finish with olive oil and a generous crack of black pepper.

FRIENDS WITH

Asparagus ribbons with pickled pink dressing p92

Carb on carb is always a good idea. You'll be dipping the peel back into the skordalia (which is an excuse to eat mashed potato with your hands) and wondering why you don't always eat mash this way. I know it looks like a lot of garlic, because it is! The starchiness of the potato dip needs it, though, and it really lifts the whole salad. Obviously garlic varies in heat level, and I'm talking about a mild, sweet, Italian-style variety, preferably grown close to where you're cooking, and even better if it's new season (at its sweetest). If you've got the time, peel the potatoes and store them and the soaking peel overnight in the fridge to help oomph up the starch in any kind of spud, giving you the fluffiest dip and the crispiest crisp (this also works when making gnocchi and mash).

Skordalia *with* asparagus *and* potato peel crisps

To make the potato peel crisps, peel the potatoes for the skordalia, reserving the peel. Cover the potato peelings with water and splash in the vinegar. Leave to soak for as long as possible.

Preheat the oven to 200°C (400°F) or 180°C (350°F) fan forced. Drain the potato peel, spin or pat dry, then toss with 1 tablespoon olive oil and ½ teaspoon salt flakes. Bake for 15–20 minutes, giving them the odd toss. Leave them on the tray to cool while you make the rest of the dish.

To make the skordalia, cut the potatoes into 3 cm (1¼ inch) chunks and drop them into a large saucepan of well-salted cold water. Bring to the boil and cook for 15 minutes or so, until potato is super soft and fall-apart fork-tender (otherwise you'll get lumps!).

Put the garlic and 1 teaspoon salt into a mortar and pestle and grind, or smush together on a chopping board with the blade of your knife on a 45 degree angle, until minced.

Drain the potato through a heatproof colander, then return to the empty saucepan, leaving to steam dry for 1–2 minutes. Add the lemon zest, garlic and salt to the potatoes and mash until smooth. Keep the colander handy.

Add ¾ cup (185 ml) olive oil and the lemon juice to the potato mixture a little at a time, whipping with a wooden spoon or flexible spatula after each juicy addition to emulsify, tasting for desired lemoniness. The texture should be saucy and smooth, and the taste like a lemony garlicky slap in the schnoz.

2 bunches (500 g) thick asparagus

1 tablespoon extra virgin olive oil

1 pinch salt flakes

GARLICKY POTATO SKORDALIA

3 large starchy potatoes, about 650 g (1 lb 7 oz)

6–7 garlic cloves

1 teaspoon salt flakes

Zest and juice of 1 lemon

¾ cup (185 ml) extra virgin olive oil

Lots of freshly ground pepper

SALT & VINEGAR POTATO PEEL CRISPS

2 tablespoons white wine vinegar

1 tablespoon extra virgin olive oil

½ teaspoon salt flakes

FINAL BITS & BOBS

1 tablespoon oregano leaves

Boil 2 cups (500 ml) of water. Snap off the woody ends of the asparagus and pop it into the handy heatproof colander in the sink. When the water has boiled, pour it over the asparagus until it just changes colour. Transfer the quick-blanched asparagus to a large bowl and toss in 1 tablespoon olive oil and a pinch of salt flakes. Leave in the bowl until ready to tiger.

To tiger the asparagus, heat the grill plate or a griddle pan over a very high heat and, when smoking hot, arrange the asparagus horizontally across the plate and cook on all sides for 2-3 minutes until some charred stripes appear and it's tender inside.

When ready to serve, schmear the potato skordalia over a platter and lay the tigered asparagus on top. Season with salt and pepper, then scatter oregano leaves and the peel crisps over and around, for dipping into the skordalia and delighting your guests.

FRIENDS WITH

Miso-roasted cauli with broad bean smash p164

You may have grown up with this dressing, or you might be looking at it and thinking, 'WHAT!?' Either way, welcome, because it's time for a retro revival. The condensed milk combined with hot English mustard is piquancy at its peak – sweet but not sickly (trust me) and sharp enough to make every mouthful sing. I love the way the eggy mimosa dances on the top of the lettuce here and, because it's oil-free, it's the kind of dressed iceberg salad that you can plonk in the middle of the table (to oohs and ahhs) and happily eat for a few hours over a long lunch. If you want further crisp iceberg tips, check out the Surf club salad (on page 106).

Mimosa lettuce *with* retro dressing

To make the condensed milk dressing, combine all of the ingredients in a bowl and mix together. Taste and season with more salt and pepper if necessary.

Drain the lettuce, remove any mangy outer leaves, trim the core flat and put the whole thing in a salad spinner. Give it a few bursts and dry well on a clean tea towel (dish towel), then transfer to the fridge to keep chilled until ready to get the party started.

To serve, use a sharp knife to slice the lettuce into four thick horizontal slabs, keeping the lettuce's structural integrity as secure as possible. You'll essentially be rebuilding the lettuce, drizzling the dressing generously in between like mortar.

Place the base of the lettuce on a round platter and grace with a generous amount of the dressing then, using a microplane, grate an egg over and sprinkle a little chive action. Top with the next slice of lettuce and add dressing, egg and chives as before. Continue these layers until the top is popped back into place. Finally, grate the last egg over the top for the crown and sprinkle with the remaining chives. Slice into wedges to serve at the table, or let the guests tong out bits to their (lettuce) heart's content.

1 hero iceberg lettuce, soaked in icy water

CONDENSED MILK DRESSING

395 g (14 oz) tin sweetened condensed milk

1 tablespoon hot English mustard (or 2 if you dare)

¾ cup (185 ml) white wine vinegar

2 teaspoons salt flakes

½ teaspoon ground white pepper

FINAL BITS & BOBS

4 eggs, hardboiled and peeled

½ cup finely sliced chives

FRIENDS WITH

Grilled peach salad with burrata and green peppercorns p60

Fattoush is a fab way of using up what you've got; be it the last of the pitas, the dukkah at the back of the cupboard, and especially that bottle of pomegranate molasses standing next to it. Dukkah-encrusted pita gives dusty dukkah you bought ages ago a second chance, because heating it will help to give it new life (or at least hide the fact that it's on its last gasp). If you have no dukkah, you're welcome to use za'atar, or just olive oil and sesame seeds if you've those handy instead. Sumac may or may not be in your pantry, and since it's mainly here for its striking scarlet sprinkle rather than make-or-break acidity, I'm cool with you subbing in sweet paprika. Got a particularly fertile pomegranate with leftovers? Why not make the cauli tabouli (see page 62)?

'Pita lid on it' fattoush

Preheat the oven to 200°C (400°F) or 180°C (350°F) fan forced. Line a baking tray with baking paper.

To make the pita lid, put dukkah and olive oil in a little bowl and stir about to combine. Place the pita on the baking tray and pour half the dukkah mixture over the pita. Flip it and pour the rest of the dukkah mixture on, making sure to scoop out every last sesame seed. Bake for 8–10 minutes until the pita is crispy and golden.

Meanwhile, in a large mortar (or on a sturdy chopping board) place the cucumbers in the firing line and smash with the pestle or the side of a rolling pin to break them up into bite-sized chunks, then transfer to a large mixing bowl. Do the same with the cherry tomatoes. Reserve the juicy mortar.

To slice the capsicum, lop off the very top end, pull out the guts and tap out the seeds. Keeping the capsicum's shape, slice into 5 mm rings. Clear the chopping board of any seeds or capsicum entrails, then peel and slice the salad onion into rings too.

Add the capsicum and onion to the cucumber in the mixing bowl, and squeeze the lemon juice over with a good sprinkle of salt and pepper.

500 g (1 lb 2 oz) Lebanese cucumbers, cut into thirds horizontally

250 g (9 oz) yellow cherry tomatoes

1 small yellow capsicum (pepper), about 270 g (9½ oz)

½ white salad onion

Juice of 1 lemon, zest reserved for dressing

Seeds of 1 pomegranate

PITA LID

1 tablespoon dukkah

2 tablespoons extra virgin olive oil, plus extra for finishing

1 large thin pita

HAYDARI DRESSING

1–2 garlic cloves

¼ teaspoon salt flakes

4 tablespoons natural yoghurt

2 tablespoons tahini

1 teaspoon honey

FINAL BITS & BOBS

1 tablespoon pomegranate molasses

1 pinch sumac (or sweet paprika!)

To make the Haydari dressing, put the garlic and salt into the juicy mortar and pestle about until it's finely smushed to a paste. Gloop in the yoghurt, tahini and honey, along with the reserved lemon zest, and stir together, then season with more salt and pepper to taste. Set aside until ready to use.

Tumble the smashed and sliced veg into your serving bowl, reserving any liquid that's pooled in the bottom. Loosen the dressing with these juices so it's nice and easy to drizzle. Finish with the pomegranate seeds, then close the pita over the salad bowl like a lid.

Pour the Haydari dressing into a nice, deep little serving bowl. Drizzle the dressing with the pomegranate molasses and a lick of extra virgin olive oil. Finish with a sprinkle of sumac (or paprika!).

This salad is all about the drama, mama. Bring it to the table like a pie, lift the pita off for exaltations, drizzle with the Haydari dressing, then close the pita lid again and let your guest of honour smash the pita through the salad with serving spoons.

FRIENDS WITH

Squashed squash on yoghurty lemon dressing p34

This is a particularly Aussie salad – familiar to those who spent summers doing Nippers (that's junior lifesaving) or any other kind of summery activity down by the beach. Usually the orange would be slipped off to the side as a bit of a half-time hit of acidity, but I've incorporated it into the combo as you might in a fennel and citrus salad, which, incidentally, could totally work here too. What you'll notice is that I've left off the olive oil until the final bits and bobs, because adding the oil early is what makes for limp lettuce. Popping it on the table is not only better for endurance, it also means people are up and about, serving themselves and each other, interacting and reminiscing about summers by the beach (or, if you're nowhere near Australia, *Home and Away*).

Surf club salad

To segment the orange, lop off the top and bottom for a steady base, then follow the line as close to the edge of the pith as possible, to unleash the flesh. Slice into each segment at a 45 degree angle (if this is your first time, don't worry: it gets easier, like learning to dive into the waves). Reserve the orange skeleton for serving.

Drain the lettuce, remove any mangy outer leaves, trim the core flat and put the whole thing in a salad spinner. Give it a few bursts and dry well on a clean tea towel (dish towel). Cut lettuce into thin wedges, keeping the core attached. Put it in a large serving bowl and tumble in the tomatoes, onion and orange and sprinkle with the parsley from a height.

Put the lemon half, orange skeleton and a bottle of extra virgin olive oil on the table along with the salt and pepper so guests can serve themselves.

1 orange

1 iceberg lettuce, soaked in cold water

250 g (9 oz) cherry tomatoes, quartered, OR 250 g (9 oz) tomatoes, cut into wedges

1 small red onion, thinly sliced

½ cup loosely packed parsley leaves, coarsely chopped

FINAL BITS & BOBS

½ lemon, for the table

Extra virgin olive oil, for the table

FRIENDS WITH
Greek-ish salad with nectarines p42

GREEN MANGO, POMELO
& HERB BŪN (PAGE 68)

PLAYLUNCH SALAD WITH
CHILLI—HONEY DRESSING
(PAGE 122)

JAPANESE SNOW SLAW
(PAGE 56)

GADO GADO PLATTER WITH
PANTRY SATAY SAUCE
(PAGE 82)

This is the kind of bouquet you'd pay a pretty penny for in a bistro, but it can equally be a posy for every day. Keep it simple and just go a punnet of mesclun with this dressing, then do what I do at home, which is ix-nay on the uss-fay and simply toss leaves in the bowl, add the dressing just before serving and call it a day. You can have perfectly crisp, chilled leaves for up to five days if you treat 'em right, siphoning off leaves for small salads as you need. Just wrap spun, undressed leaves carefully in paper towel and put them in a container or loosely tied bag in the fridge.

Bistro bouquet *with* mignonette dressing

1 large soft lettuce such as oak leaf or butterhead (or assorted leaves)

½ bunch radishes, about 125 g (4½ oz), finely sliced and soaked in cold water

SMALL AND SWEET (MIGNONETTE) DRESSING

2 golden shallots (see page 17), finely diced

1 teaspoon caster (superfine) sugar

2 tablespoons red wine vinegar

½ teaspoon salt flakes

1 tablespoon just-boiled water

1 teaspoon freshly cracked black pepper

¼ cup (60 ml) extra virgin olive oil

FINAL BITS & BOBS

½ cup finely snipped chives and dill sprigs, or other soft herb leaves (such as parsley)

10 g (⅜ oz) edible flowers (optional but excellent)

To make the dressing, grab a clean jar and put the shallot, caster sugar, vinegar, salt and water into the base of the jar. Close the lid and give it a good shake together until the sugar dissolves and the shallots start blushing. Add the rest of the dressing ingredients and shake again like a polaroid picture, to combine. Leave to develop and relax for around half an hour before serving, if you can.

Use your hands to separate the lettuce into its leaves and pop into a large bowl of cold water to soak. After 15 minutes, drain the chilled, refreshed leaves and spin in a salad spinner or clean tea towel (outside!), then lay on clean, dry paper towel to capture any final moisture.

When ready to serve, pour a third of the dressing into the base of a wide, high-sided salad bowl. Build the leafy bouquet by starting with the larger leaves at the base, resting on the sides, then assembling the smaller leaves at the front. Artfully arrange the radish slices poking out from between the leaves and sprinkle with the chives and dill, or other soft herbs, and edible flowers, if using. Serve the extra dressing at the table or store in the fridge for up to a week. Scoop a little dressing with the base of the leaves as you dish it out.

FRIENDS WITH

Triple cherry Caprese with bright basil oil p47

Grilling lettuce brings out its natural sweetness, and creates lovely dimension and contrast between the crisp crunch of well-refreshed lettuce heart and the bittersweet charred bits on the exterior. A stick blender is best here, for control, but any blender will do. You could always shortcut the aïoli by whizzing some anchovies and garlic through some whole egg mayo. You can also make this plant-based by making an aquafaba aïoli and whizzing capers into it for extra briney bounce, and then using a planty cheese or grated hazelnuts or macadamias for the cloud instead. I've made extra aïoli because it goes with everything, so serve it alongside the salad, for extra drizzling and dipping.

Grilled cos wedges *with* anchovy aïoli

To make the aïoli, put the egg yolks, garlic, anchovies, mustard, vinegar and a tablespoon of water into the base of a blender, or a tall jug, if using a stick blender. Blitz to a paste, checking that the garlic has fully broken down.

Combine the oils in a small jug, then dribble the combo in, drip by drip to start, while constantly blending. Once you see a colour change and the mixture starts to emulsify and thicken, you can pour in the oils in a slow and steady stream. When it becomes very thick at the end, add the lemon zest and juice, and thin with another tablespoon of water so that it's drizzleable. Taste and season with pepper, then blitz until super smooth. Decant into a serving jug and set aside.

Heat a clean barbecue grill or grill plate on high.

Cut the cos lengthways and, when ready to grill, brush it and the baguette slices sparingly with olive oil.

Place the cos cut-side down on the grill and cook for a minute or two without moving (you want the char marks). The baguette slices will be ready to flip after a minute.

Remove items from the grill, rub the baguette with the halved garlic clove and place on a serving plate, along with the cos, charred-side up. Pour half the anchovy aïoli over, then top with a puffy cloud of finely grated parmesan and a generous sprinkle of chives. Finely grate lemon zest over and one last crack of pepper for good measure.

Pour the rest of the aïoli into a jug or bowl and pop it on the table so that eaters can help themselves.

4 baby cos (romaine) lettuce, bases trimmed and outer leaves removed
¼ cup (60 ml) extra virgin olive oil

ANCHOVY AÏOLI

2 egg yolks
2 garlic cloves
6–8 anchovy fillets
1 heaped teaspoon dijon mustard
1 tablespoon white wine vinegar
⅔ cup (170 ml) grapeseed oil
⅓ cup (80 ml) extra virgin olive oil
Zest and juice of 1 lemon

GARLIC CROSTINI

1 small baguette, thinly sliced on the diagonal
1 garlic clove, halved for rubbing

FINAL BITS & BOBS

25 g (1 oz) parmesan cheese
¼ cup (20 g) finely snipped chives
Zest of 1 lemon

FRIENDS WITH

Twinkling tomatoes with milk kefir dressing p32

This is like a spring roll, in a salad! Oh, man, it is SO good. If you're taking this to a party, make sure to keep the chips separate and wait for them to cool, or cover with paper towel or loosely scrunched foil rather than a lid if they're still warm. Store-bought plum jam varies in sweetness, so add extra salt and vinegar if you need to balance the flavours. I love using mung bean noodles, but rice vermicelli noodles will work. Spring roll wrappers are easy substitutes – I just prefer the golden brown of a fried wonton wrapper rather than the mild yellow of the fried spring roll wrapper. You could also use prawn crackers or crunchy noodles if you don't have time to fry.

Rock 'n' roll salad *with* plum dressing *and* crispy bits

Make the plum sauce dipper dressing by whisking all of the ingredients together in a large bowl.

Cook the noodles according to packet instructions, then snip into shorter lengths.

Add the noodles, spring onion, carrot, mushroom, bean sprouts, water chestnuts and wombok to the dressing in the bowl, tossing to coat.

Cut the wonton wrappers into quarter triangles. Heat 1 cm (⅜ inch) of oil in a medium saucepan to 180°C (350°F) – a piece of wrapper should go golden in 20 seconds – and cook wrapper quarters in batches for about 1–2 minutes until a light golden brown. Drain on paper towel.

Transfer the salad ingredients onto a platter, scatter with chilli, coriander leaves and crispy fried shallots, and finish with the crispy wonton wrappers just before serving.

50 g (1¾ oz) mung bean or rice vermicelli noodles

2–3 spring onions (scallions), julienned into ribbons

1 carrot, finely julienned

6–8 fresh shiitake mushrooms, finely sliced

125 g (4½ oz) bean sprouts, soaked in water

140 g (5 oz) tin water chestnuts, sliced

250 g (9 oz) finely sliced wombok (Chinese cabbage)

PLUM SAUCE DIPPER DRESSING

¾ cup (250 g) plum jam

2 tablespoons sweet chilli sauce

2 tablespoons rice wine vinegar

2 tablespoons soy sauce

2 tablespoons sesame oil

1 tablespoon peanut oil

2 garlic cloves, minced

1 thumb ginger, grated

½ teaspoon five spice

2 tablespoons coriander (cilantro) stems, very finely chopped

¾ teaspoon salt flakes

FINAL BITS & BOBS

10 wonton wrappers

Neutral oil, for shallow-frying (peanut or rice bran works here)

1 long red chilli, finely sliced

1 cup loosely packed coriander (cilantro) leaves

Crispy fried shallots

FRIENDS WITH

Playlunch salad p122

This needs a sweet but tart apple, so something like a JAZZ works well. Poppyseeds aren't just textural, they also infuse a sweet, nutty, lightly aniseedy flavour into the dressing. I like making this dressing in a jar, because you'll probably still have enough left over for tomorrow's salad. Just shake it back up, because it'll separate again. Wombok does wonders for slaws because it takes far less time to soften and has a milder, sweeter flavour than traditional winter cabbages, but if you've only got white cabbage at your disposal, shred it and massage with a little salt to soften it.

Wombok slaw *with* sweet poppyseed dressing

To make the dressing, put all of the ingredients into a jar and give it a cocktail-bar shake. Taste and season with freshly ground black pepper, and set aside in the jar for the flavours to develop and the poppy seeds to rehydrate.

In a large bowl, combine the red cabbage, wombok, onion and apple. Give the dressing another good shake and pour it over the salad, tossing again to coat generously.

Transfer to a serving dish and scatter with parsley and chives. Serve immediately.

500 g (1 lb 2 oz) finely shredded red cabbage

500 g (1 lb 2 oz) finely shredded wombok (Chinese cabbage)

½ small red onion, finely sliced

2 tart red apples, julienned into matchsticks, tossed in lemon juice

HONEY & POPPYSEED DRESSING

½ small red onion, finely chopped or grated

2 teaspoons hot English mustard

½ cup (125 ml) apple cider vinegar

2 tablespoons runny honey

2 teaspoons poppy seeds

1 teaspoon salt flakes

½ cup (125 ml) neutral oil (I like grapeseed or sunflower oil here)

FINAL BITS & BOBS

1 handful parsley leaves, finely sliced

2 tablespoons finely sliced chives

FRIENDS WITH

Celery and blueberry salad with ranch dressing p124

Crunch, sweetness, juiciness in a magic midsummer combo that's familiar yet refreshingly different (and differently refreshing)! Get ready for a double flavour-bomb with the sesame–spring onion oil and the tahini–miso cream. Shiso leaves are special for flavour and colour, but coriander could be swapped in. Daikon is an underutilised vegetable. Plating here is a little more conceptual than you need to do at home: feel free to do rounds on the mandolin for both cukes and daikon, or peel strips of both on a speed or julienne peeler then toss together with the dressings and sprinkle to finish.

Cucumber & daikon sheets
with tahini–miso dressing

700 g (1 lb 9 oz) daikon, soaked in cold water

125 g (4½ oz) baby cucumbers, thinly sliced into discs

TAHINI–MISO CREAM

1 thumb ginger, grated

¼ cup (65 g) tahini

1 tablespoon white miso paste

1 tablespoon sesame oil

1 teaspoon maple syrup

SESAME–SPRING ONION OIL

½ cup (125 ml) peanut oil

2 spring onions (scallions), finely chopped

1 garlic clove, minced

1 tablespoon sesame oil

½ teaspoon sugar

1 teaspoon salt flakes

FINAL BITS & BOBS

1 tablespoon furikake (rice seasoning)

½ teaspoon salt flakes

10 g (⅜ oz) red shiso leaves (optional but excellent)

To make the tahini–miso cream, squeeze the ginger pulp in your fist over a medium bowl to extract the juice, reserving the fuzz for the sesame–spring onion oil. Add the remaining ingredients and whisk together until emulsified, using a little cold water if necessary to make it the consistency of pouring cream.

Drain and dry the daikon. Using a sharp knife, slice the daikon into 8 cm (3½ inch) lengths. Then use a mandolin (or the knife) to shave sheets of daikon, dropping the slices into the cold water again to firm up.

To make the sesame–spring onion oil, start by heating the peanut oil in a small saucepan. Put the remaining ingredients, including the reserved ginger fuzz, into a heatproof bowl. When the oil is smoking hot and shimmering (but not actually smoking!), pour it over the ingredients in the bowl and leave to bubble, bubble, with little toil or trouble.

Swish the tahini–miso cream onto the base of a shallow serving plate, then arrange the daikon sheets over the top and scatter with cucumber discs. Sprinkle with furikake, drizzle with sesame–spring onion oil and salt flakes. Finish with shiso leaves, if using.

FRIENDS WITH

Gado gado platter with pantry satay sauce p82

A retro prawn cocktail screams holidays and celebrations, especially when mixed with tropical fruit, which totally works. This salad benefits from a firm avocado, such as a Shepard, which will hold its shape better than a Hass or Reed. The dressing is an Aussie take on Thousand Island and has yoghurt inside, so why not call it an archipelago! Buy prawns frozen and thaw as needed – they're snap-frozen on the boat. If you don't want to use prawns, you could use other seafood such as crayfish, marron, bugs or scampi, or sub in firm tofu and lychees (with fysh sauce for funk) as a vego option.

Tropical prawn salad *with* archipelago dressing

Spin dry the lettuce and chop the leaves into 3 cm (1¼ inch) chunks. Cut the cheeks off the mango and then gently remove the skin with a knife or large sharp spoon. This will leave you with two cheeks, which can then be cubed. Peel the pineapple and cut this into cubes too.

To make the dressing, combine all of the ingredients in a bowl. Taste and season with salt and pepper. You can keep the salad and dressing separate until you're just about to serve.

Cut the avocado in half, remove the halves from the skin with a spoon, use the back of the spoon to smooth over any mushy spots, and then cut into cubes. Drizzle some extra lemon juice over the avo cubes to prevent them from discolouring.

Arrange the salad ingredients, including the prawns and mint, on a platter, then drizzle with the dressing. Sprinkle with chives and serve with lemon cheeks, preferably while wearing a kaftan or Hawaiian shirt.

2 baby cos (romaine) lettuces, soaked in cold water

1 firm but ripe mango

½ ripe pineapple

1 firm but ripe avocado (something like a Shepard will be best)

500 g (1 lb 2 oz) cooked and peeled prawns (tails removed)

½ bunch mint, leaves picked

ARCHIPELAGO DRESSING

⅓ cup (85 g) sour cream

⅓ cup (85 g) natural yoghurt

1½ tablespoons tomato sauce (ketchup)

1–2 teaspoons hot sauce

2 tablespoons Kewpie mayonnaise

1 tablespoon extra virgin olive oil

Juice of half a lemon, plus extra for the avocado

½ teaspoon salt flakes

¼ teaspoon freshly cracked black pepper

FINAL BITS & BOBS

2 tablespoons finely chopped chives

Lemon cheeks

FRIENDS WITH

Fruit salad with zesty dressing and salty—sweet macadamias p67

These are the ingredients you'd expect to see in a '90s lunchbox: celery sticks, Granny Smith apple slices and plenty of peanut butter. What works so well here is the freshness of the fruit and veg against the roasted peanuts, with the sweet–sour–salty balance of the dressing. To get that super satisfying crunch on your celery sticks, chop into lengths as soon as you get them home and pop into cold water in a lidded tub in the fridge, ready to go. Don't forget to save the celery tops and stumps for the freezer bag for making stocks. If you'd prefer to keep this planty, pull the fish sauce out for fysh sauce or add an extra half teaspoon of salt flakes.

Playlunch salad *with* chilli–honey dressing

To make the dressing, measure out 1 tablespoon of just-boiled water into a heatproof bowl, then use the same (now hot!) tablespoon to scoop out the honey, then pour another tablespoon of just-boiled water into the tablespoon and stir about to make a honey syrup. Pop the chilli, lime juice and fish sauce into the bowl, along with the peanut oil and salt and stir again. Taste and adjust flavours for balance, then leave to infuse.

Slice the cheeks off the apples and thinly slice into half-moon slivers. Pop into water with a splash of extra lime juice in a salad spinner, along with the chopped celery, coriander sprigs and spring onion.

When ready to serve, spin the apples, celery, coriander and spring onion dry. Transfer to a mixing bowl with the baby spinach and pour the dressing over, tossing about to coat.

Transfer to a serving platter or bowl and scatter with the chopped peanuts and serve with lime cheeks on the side.

2 tart green apples

½ large bunch celery (4 stalks), sliced on the diagonal into 1 cm (⅜ inch) chunks

¼ bunch coriander (cilantro) sprigs

2 spring onions (scallions), finely sliced on the bias

1½ cups loosely packed baby spinach leaves, about 50 g (1¾ oz)

CHILLI–HONEY DRESSING

2 tablespoons just-boiled water

1 tablespoon honey

1 green chilli, very finely diced

Juice of 1 lime, plus extra for apple

1 tablespoon fish sauce

1 tablespoon peanut oil

½ teaspoon salt flakes

FINAL BITS & BOBS

½ cup (80 g) roasted peanuts, coarsely chopped

Lime cheeks

FRIENDS WITH

Rock 'n' roll salad with plum dressing and crispy bits p114

This salad goes all in on North American flavours, with a blue cheese ranch and mapled pecans that balance out the funky creamy saltiness perfectly. I like having garlic powder in my salad dressing arsenal, especially for creamy ones, because it cuts through anything too rich with just the right kind of piquancy. My preference is the organic garlic powder with a green lid, which you'll find in health food shops. Berries, particularly blueberries, are worth keeping in mind for adding pops of acidity, sweetness and colour into salads – sweet and savoury! Blueberries are always best served chilled.

Celery *and* blueberry salad *with* ranch dressing

Finely shave fennel, celery stalks, celery heart and onion with a mandolin, keeping with the shape of the fennel and the onion, and shaving the celery on the bias. Pop into a salad spinner with the celery leaves, fennel fronds, parsley and plenty of cold water with a splash of apple cider vinegar and put it into the fridge while you make the dressing and maple the pecans.

Preheat the oven to 180°C (350°F) or 160°C (320°F) fan forced. Line a small baking tray with baking paper.

To make the salted-maple pecans, toss pecans together with the maple syrup and a pinch of salt flakes and spread onto the baking tray. Toast in the oven for 5 minutes, keeping an eye on them to make sure they don't burn. Take out and set aside to cool and crisp up.

To make the dressing, put all of the ingredients except the chives into a small blender and blitz until smooth. Fold in the chives and set aside.

Just before serving, halve the blueberries horizontally to reveal the tiny star inside.

Drain and spin the veg. To make it super dry and dressing-ready, scatter the veg across a clean tea towel (dish towel), roll it up and pat like you're drying off a toddler at the beach.

Tumble the veg and blueberries together into a shallow serving bowl. Drizzle with the dressing (if you've got extra, leave it nearby in a jug), scatter with salted-maple pecans and extra chives, and finish with a flourish of extra virgin olive oil and a final sprinkle of salt flakes and freshly cracked pepper.

1 small fennel bulb, fronds reserved

2 celery stalks

1 celery heart, yellow leaves reserved

1 small white salad onion, sliced in half

½ cup loosely packed parsley leaves, roughly chopped, reserving the stems

2 tablespoons apple cider vinegar

125 g (4½ oz) large blueberries

SALTED-MAPLE PECANS

¼ cup (25 g) pecans

1 tablespoon maple syrup

1 pinch salt flakes

BLITZED BLUE CHEESE & BUTTERMILK RANCH DRESSING

90 g (3¼ oz) blue cheese

1 tablespoon extra virgin olive oil, plus extra for finishing

2 tablespoons apple cider vinegar

¼ cup (65 g) sour cream

½ cup (125 ml) buttermilk

¼ teaspoon salt flakes

1 teaspoon maple syrup

½ teaspoon freshly cracked black pepper

2 tablespoons finely chopped reserved parsley stems

Scant ¼ teaspoon garlic powder

2 tablespoons finely chopped chives, plus extra for garnish

FRIENDS WITH

Wombok slaw with sweet poppyseed dressing p116

This is a salad that welcomes seasonal replacements: if asparagus isn't around, you can sub blanched green beans or broccolini bits; flip frisée into any green leaf to hand. Breakfast radishes are the long ones. If you can't find them, use the regular squat ones. Blue cheese is the bit that stays – the umami punch – and it's up to you whether that punch is a roquefort right-hander or a blue Castello left hook. Either way, it's a knockout. This dressing would be beautiful as a light sauce over proteins, tossed through new season baby potatoes, or in a dippy bowl as a vego bagna cauda with crudité vegetables.

Asparagus *and* radish salad *with* caper vinaigrette

Put a saucepan of well-salted water on the stove to boil, then snap off the asparagus ends then cut or snap the spears into 2 cm (¾ inch) batons on the bias. Drop them into the boiling water to cook for 2 minutes or until lurid green and tender. Drain and plunge into cold water to stop the cooking process.

Finely slice the radishes vertically on a mandolin and drop in a little bowl of cold water until they snap to attention.

Drain the lettuce and radish, then spin-dry together and lay on paper towel until ready to deploy.

To make the vinaigrette, combine all of the ingredients in a small bowl and whisk together with a fork. Taste and add salt and pepper if needed.

Assemble the salad, starting with the lettuce and radish, then add the asparagus and blobs of blue cheese (use a teaspoon to crack into it and keep your fingers from melting into it too much). Drizzle with the caper vinaigrette at the table.

250 g (9 oz) asparagus spears

1 bunch breakfast radishes, about 250 g (9 oz)

1 small frisée lettuce (endive), soaked in cold water

80 g (2¾ oz) blue cheese (such as roquefort or blue Castello – whatever floats your boat)

CAPER VINAIGRETTE

1 golden shallot (see page 17), finely diced (about 1 heaped tablespoon)

¼ cup (60 ml) extra virgin olive oil

2 tablespoons white wine vinegar

1 small garlic clove, minced

1 heaped teaspoon seeded mustard

1 tablespoon finely chopped tarragon leaves

1 tablespoon finely chopped parsley leaves

1 tablespoon capers, rinsed, drained and finely chopped

½ teaspoon salt flakes

¼ teaspoon freshly cracked pepper

FRIENDS WITH

Radish & potato salad with creamy tarragon dressing p44

Cooler *Days*

I love roasting grapes: the flavour becomes magically meaty and broody, which makes them a perfect candidate for a trans-seasonal salad. You can serve this up in autumn with the grapes cooled, or keep them warm for winter. The gorgonzola pops against the acidity of the sticky sherry vinegar, which is reminiscent of a sticky wine you'd drink with a cheese board. If you're in the market for sherry vinegar, I like Jerez, or if you can find a PX (Pedro Ximénez) vinegar, charge at it like a bull at a red rag! Roasting the radicchio, and including a creamy, funky cheese plus acidic dressing, helps to mitigate its bitterness.

Hot cheeseboard salad *with* honey–walnut dressing

Preheat the oven to 220°C (430°F) or 200°C (400°F) fan forced. Pop the walnuts on a baking tray and straight into the preheating oven, then set the timer for 5 minutes. Check on them at this point and give them a few more minutes if they need it, as heating speeds will vary.

Make the sticky sherry vinegar by popping the vinegar and honey in a small saucepan, bringing to a boil, then dropping to a simmer for 10 minutes or until glossy and syrupy. Give it the odd check to make sure it doesn't burn. When you've got about ¼ cup (60 ml) left, turn off the heat. Leave in the pot.

Cut the radicchio into wedges, still attached at the stalk. Tear cavolo nero off its stalk, then roughly tear again into fork-sized flaps. Tear the grapes off their vine and into a baking dish along with the shallot wedges and radicchio. Stir together the olive oil, sherry vinegar and honey to form a glossy drizz and pour over the tray, using your hands to help twist and coat. Pop the cavolo nero on a second tray and dress with a tablespoon of olive oil and a sprinkle of salt flakes.

Transfer both into the oven, the purple tray on top and the green below. After 5 minutes, pull out the cavolo nero tray (crispy and still deep green) and remove the radicchio from the top of the purple tray. Roast the grapes and shallots for another 10 minutes until the grapes are blistered and shiny and the shallots have completely relaxed.

Pour any remaining tray juices into the sticky sherry vinegar to loosen (if there aren't any juices, splash in a teaspoon or so of water), then reheat slightly to help incorporate.

Arrange the roasted veg and grapes on a serving platter. Pour the sticky sherry vinegar over the top of the arranged fruit and veg. Crumble the gorgonzola on top, along with the roasted walnuts, and finish with a final flourish of extra virgin olive oil and the salt and pepper.

1 head radicchio, about 200 g (7 oz), trimmed

½ bunch cavolo nero, about 150 g (5½ oz)

250 g (9 oz) red seedless grapes

2 banana shallots (see page 17), sliced into wedges

¼ cup (60 ml) extra virgin olive oil, plus extra for drizzling

1 tablespoon sherry vinegar

1 tablespoon runny honey

STICKY SHERRY VINEGAR

½ cup (125 ml) sherry vinegar

¼ cup (90 g) runny honey

FINAL BITS & BOBS

½ cup (60 g) fresh walnuts

100 g (3½ oz) gorgonzola dolce

2 tablespoons extra virgin olive oil

½ teaspoon salt flakes

¼ teaspoon ground black pepper

FRIENDS WITH

Kipflers and green beans dressed by Almondine p214

In this salad, PG (parsley and garlic) paste is the marinade AND the dressing, the dual fuel that's full of flav. You can eat this warm or cold – as more pasta or more salad. The quickly blanched calamari's terrific texturally against the al dente shells, and I quite enjoy the play of an oceanic pasta shape and protein. Don't overcook the calamari – it's a quick in-and-out situation. If you'd prefer to keep this plant based, sub in cooked chickpeas or big white beans.

Calamari *and* shell pasta salad

350 g fresh calamari, sliced into 5 mm
  (¼ inch) rings

½ cup (85 g) small capers, rinsed and
  drained

200 g (7 oz) sugar plum cherry tomatoes,
  quartered

200 g (7 oz) small shell pasta

PG DRESSING

1 bunch parsley

1 garlic bulb (about 10 cloves),
  cloves separated and peeled

Zest and juice of 1 lemon

1 cup (250 ml) extra virgin olive oil,
  plus extra for splashing

1 teaspoon salt flakes

FINAL BITS & BOBS

Lemon wedges (optional)

Bring a large saucepan of well-salted water to the boil.

Meanwhile, make the PG dressing. Pick half a packed cup of the smaller parsley leaves and set aside for the garnish. Put the rest of the unpicked parsley bunch (stalks and all), garlic cloves, lemon zest and juice, olive oil and salt into a blender. Blitz to a verdant green paste and transfer to a mixing bowl.

When the water is boiling, add the calamari and cook for 30 seconds, then scoop out, tap to drain and dump into the PG dressing, along with the capers and tomatoes.

Wait until the water comes back to the boil, throw in the pasta shells and cook for 2 minutes less than suggested on the packet. Drain and rinse, then toss onto a tray with a splash of extra olive oil and spread out in one layer to cool down quickly and dry out a bit. Swoosh off the tray into the PG dressing, along with the reserved parsley leaves, and toss everything together.

Tumble onto a platter and serve with lemon wedges, if using, and some freshly cracked pepper.

FRIENDS WITH

Sautéed squash and zucchini with
pangrattato p26, Tricolour piperade with
muffuletta dressing p174

A salad featuring hardboiled eggs screams any-time-of-day option, from 8 am to 8 pm. You may have tasted fermented black bean as a sauce in Cantonese cookery, but if it's new to you, imagine a nuttier Vegemite (or whatever 'yeast extract spread' is endemic to you). Fermented black bean is usually sold vac-packed; it's preserved in salt, which can be intimidating at first, but once you get your head around rinsing and soaking, you'll be able to unlock unbelievable umami in your dishes (and it's got great shelf-life, too). You could also repurpose leftover roast veg through this salad.

Eggplant *and* capsicum *with* fermented black bean dressing

Preheat the oven to 200°C (400°F) or 180°C (350°F) fan forced.

Toss the capsicum with half the neutral oil. Spread out capsicum on a baking tray, reserving the oily bowl. Toss eggplant in the rest of the oil, then lay on a second baking tray. Roast for 15 minutes, then give the eggplants a flip and continue cooking both trays for another 15 minutes until the skin of the capsicum has started to blacken and blister and the eggplant is golden and soft in the middle. The eggplant may need another 5–10 minutes after the capsicum comes out to really get some colour on it (more is always more with eggplant).

Make the dressing by rinsing the black beans in warm water, then covering with more warm water to soak for 5 minutes. Meanwhile, pop the neutral oil and sliced shallots into a small saucepan and heat until the shallot starts to soften and turn slightly golden. Add the garlic and ginger and toss about until deeply aromatic. Chuck in the soaked and drained black beans, soy sauce, rice wine, sesame oil and honey, and toss about to combine. Bring back to a sizzle, then switch off the heat. Taste and season with salt and pepper.

Boil the eggs in a small saucepan, liberally covered with cold water (about 3 cm/1¼ inch above the top of the eggs). When the water's boiling, set a timer for 6 minutes. Cool immediately by running under the tap or popping them into a bowl of cold water. When cooled enough to handle, peel and set aside.

Put the capsicum (no need to peel) and eggplant on a platter. Cut the boiled eggs in half and nestle them into the salad. Drizzle with the dressing and scatter spring onion on top.

1 kg (2 lb 4 oz) mixed sweet capsicums (peppers), cored and sliced into rounds

¼ cup (60 ml) neutral oil (I like grapeseed or peanut here)

3–4 Japanese eggplants (aubergines), about 500 g (1 lb 2 oz), sliced into 1 cm (⅜ inch) discs

4 eggs

FERMENTED BLACK BEAN DRESSING

1 heaped tablespoon salted fermented black beans

¼ cup (60 ml) neutral oil (I like grapeseed or peanut here)

4 golden shallots (see page 17), thinly sliced

2 garlic cloves, thinly sliced

1 thumb ginger, grated

2 tablespoons light soy sauce

1 tablespoon shaoxing rice wine

2 tablespoons sesame oil

2 tablespoons honey

¼ teaspoon ground white pepper

FINAL BITS & BOBS

2 spring onions (scallions), finely sliced

FRIENDS WITH

Agrodolce roasted brassicas with macadamia cream p222

Frisée and witlof are bitter greens that are at their best in autumn, which is exactly when you'll find figs at their most juicy and jammy. Grilling them makes them even jammier, so if you get a disappointing fig, sprinkle with a little sugar, grill and watch the magic happen. If you don't plan on serving right away, prep everything but keep the elements separate until ready to serve. You can even wrap the leaves in a clean tea towel (dish towel) and chill in the fridge. Chervil offers a lovely gentle anise flavour, but if you can't find any and have some tarragon handy, it'll be perfect here – otherwise any soft herb will work: dill, parsley, even Thai or holy basil, come to think of it!

Frisée, witlof & grilled fig *with* goat's cheese

Heat a heavy-based frying pan until smoking. Carefully lay some baking paper on top, then sprinkle a little sugar, if using, over the cut fig faces and pop the figs face down on the paper. The figs will bubble away and release some liquid: watch for the bubbles to dissipate and the sugars to caramelise, which takes 3–4 minutes. Transfer to a plate face-side up until ready to serve. The figs will release some juice while they cool, so be sure to drain it off into the vinaigrette or drizzle it right over the salad.

Drain and spin the witlof and frisée.

To make the vinaigrette, whisk all of the ingredients together in a shallow serving bowl and season to taste with extra salt and pepper if need be.

Gently fold the vinaigrette through the leaves, then top with figs, hazelnuts and blobs of goat's cheese. Finish with chervil, from a height, and a final flourish of extra olive oil.

1 teaspoon sugar (optional but useful)

4–6 firm but heavy figs, halved

4 yellow witlof (chicory), trimmed and soaked in chilled water

1 frisée lettuce (endive), trimmed and soaked in chilled water

SEEDED MUSTARD VINAIGRETTE

1 tablespoon chardonnay vinegar

1 teaspoon seeded mustard

1 teaspoon runny honey

2 tablespoons extra virgin olive oil, plus extra for drizzling

½ teaspoon salt flakes

¼ teaspoon freshly cracked black pepper

FINAL BITS & BOBS

¼ cup (30 g) roasted hazelnuts, chopped

50 g (1¾ oz) fresh goat's cheese

½ bunch chervil, tufts picked

FRIENDS WITH

Honeyed butternut risoni salad with marinated feta p163

AGRODOLCE ROASTED BRASSICAS (PAGE 222)

MISO-ROASTED CAULI WITH BROAD BEAN SMASH (PAGE 164)

PISTOU-ROASTED RADISHES
WITH LENTILS (PAGE 142)

PIQUANT PANTRY SALAD WITH
A FEW GREEN BITS (PAGE 202)

If kimchi is always in your fridge – as it is in mine – this is a good way to use it up and extend it. If you can't find pineapple, try a firm pear (especially nashi). The spicy sizzle drizzle can go over anything from steamed fish and greens to wok-tossed brocc or other greens. If using tinned pineapple, it's sweeter, so you'll need to add more of the salty wombok run-off. If you want extra funk, add a splash or two of fish sauce into the dressing. Don't forget to scoop in the juice from the pineapple you've sliced or use pineapple juice from the tin if deploying the canned stuff (watch that you buy the one 'in juice' not 'syrup').

Wombok quick-chi salad

½ wombok (Chinese cabbage), about 500 g (1 lb 2 oz)

1 cup (100 g) kimchi, coarsely chopped, juices reserved

1 tablespoon gochujang paste

450 g (1 lb) tinned pineapple, drained and juice reserved, or 1 small pineapple, peeled and roughly cubed

4 spring onions (scallions), cut into 5 cm (2 inch) lengths and julienned

1 teaspoon salt flakes

SPICY SIZZLE DRIZZLE

1 long red chilli, thinly sliced

2 garlic cloves, thinly sliced

2 tablespoons fried shallots

¼ cup (60 ml) peanut oil

QUICK-CHI DRESSING

1 tablespoon oyster sauce

1 tablespoon light soy sauce

1 tablespoon rice wine vinegar

1 tablespoon sesame oil

Remove and discard the core of the wombok and cut it into 8 wedges with the grain. Then cut against the grain into 2 cm (¾ inch) fork-friendly flaps.

Massage wombok, kimchi, gochujang, pineapple and spring onions together with the salt and kimchi and pineapple juices to help break down the wombok cells. Set aside for 20 minutes, then drain and squeeze the wombok with your hands very tightly, reserving the run-off for the dressing.

Put the wombok mixture into a large mixing bowl, ready for the sizzle drizzle.

To make the spicy sizzle drizzle, put the chilli, garlic and fried shallots in a small heatproof bowl, then heat the peanut oil in a small saucepan until very hot. Pour the hot oil over the aromats in the bowl and allow to infuse for a minute.

For the quick-chi dressing, whisk together the oyster sauce, soy sauce, rice wine vinegar and sesame oil. Add some of the wombok run-off liquid and taste. Keep adding more liquid to your preference – it should taste slightly saltier than you'd expect, as it'll be spread over a lot of volume.

Stir the dressing through the mixing bowl of wombok and bits. Pour the slightly cooled drizzle over the bowl of wombok 'quick-chi' and toss about to coat. Transfer to a serving bowl and dig in.

FRIENDS WITH

Cucumber corkscrews with gochujang dressing p78

Pickled grapes are such a fun thing to have on platters and boards – like a sweet–sour pop of puce – and they're especially excellent for autumn salads. If grapes aren't around, you could do this with pitted cherry halves or even cherry tomatoes. Seek out the radish bunches with the bushiest, brightest green tops. If they're not forthcoming, use a handful more of the wild rocket as your pistou leaf. Lentils make this salad extra protein-rich and meaty – a perfectly substantial addition if catering for vegetarian eaters (make it vegan with maple in the dressing). You could use tinned brown lentils, but they can be a bit mushy, so it is worth taking the time to soak and cook from scratch.

Pistou-roasted radishes *with* lentils

Preheat the oven to 200°C (400°F) or 180°C (350°F) fan forced.

Rinse the lentils well. Put them in a medium saucepan with the tarragon and parsley stems and the red onion skin. Pour in 3 cups (750 ml) of water, then bring to the boil. Drop the heat to a simmer, then cook for 20–30 minutes until tender, which you can check by squashing a lentil between your fingers to check for any residual chalkiness through the middle.

When the lentils are done, drain through a heatproof colander, discarding the herb stems and onion skin. Rinse again under cold water and leave in the colander to drain, dry and cool.

Cut the larger radishes in half, leaving the root end and a little of the green stem attached for decorative effect. Cut any very large radishes into quarters.

Toss the radish and red onion wedges with the olive oil. Spread on a baking tray and whack into the oven for 20 minutes.

Meanwhile, make the radish tops pistou. Soak the radish tops well (watch out for grit!) and spin them dry. Blitz the tops with the garlic, salt flakes and the reserved tarragon and parsley leaves (keeping the smaller leaves aside for the dressing) in a food processor until a rough paste forms, then add the olive oil and pulse to combine.

After 20 minutes, once the radishes and onions have started to blister and shrivel, pull them out of the oven, then scoop half the pistou onto the tray and toss about to coat. Return to the oven to roast for a further 5 minutes.

½ cup (105 g) dried beluga lentils

4 tarragon stems, leaves picked and reserved for dressing

½ bunch parsley, stems and leaves separated, leaves reserved for dressing

2 red onions, cut into 1 cm (⅜ inch) wedges, skin reserved

2 bunches radishes, about 500 g (1 lb 2 oz), tops reserved for pistou

2 tablespoons extra virgin olive oil, plus extra for finishing

RADISH TOPS PISTOU

2 garlic cloves

1 teaspoon salt flakes

¼ cup (60 ml) extra virgin olive oil

PICKLED RED ONION
& GRAPE DRESSING

1 tablespoon honey

½ teaspoon salt flakes

¼ cup (60 ml) sherry vinegar

½ red onion, finely sliced with the grain

300 g (10½ oz) crimson seedless grapes, halved

1 tablespoon dijon mustard

½ teaspoon freshly ground pepper

FINAL BITS & BOBS

100 g (3½ oz) baby rocket (arugula)

FRIENDS WITH

Hot pink pear salad with zippy kale and ricotta p188

To make the dressing, whisk the honey, salt flakes and vinegar in a medium bowl to make a syrup, then add the onion and grapes and toss to coat. Set aside for 5–10 minutes to quickle. Finely chop the reserved tarragon and parsley leaves.

When the quickle is ready, pour off the pickling liquor into a clean mixing bowl and whisk in the mustard, chopped tarragon and parsley and the pepper. Taste and season with more salt and pepper, if needed, then reunite the pickled grapes and onions with the mixture.

To serve, toss the roasted radish and onion through the warm lentils, along with any pan juices and the remaining pistou. At the last minute, fold in the rocket. Pour the pickled red onion and grape dressing over the top, finishing with the reserved herbs, a final drizzle of olive oil and a sprinkle of salt flakes from a height.

Fine, yes, this IS another play on the feta tray bake AND yet another roasted cauli salad, but this time it's all about that golden raisin dressing ... make it rain! You could use currants or regular sultanas instead – any dried droop will do! Parcooking the cauli will ensure it's always cooked through. You could use other beans – whatever you have in the pantry – or even cook dry beans from scratch. It is a bit of a 'complete meal' salad, and perfect if you've got vegos coming around. If you want the feta to melt and be a bit more mushy, use Danish feta. For firmer 'bits', use a Greek one. You could even blob with marinated Persian feta as a finisher if that's what you have.

Baked cauli & feta salad *with* golden raisin dressing

Preheat the oven to 200°C (400°F) or 180°C (350°F) fan forced.

Put cauliflower in a heatproof bowl and cover with just-boiled water. Leave to par-cook for 1 minute. Drain, then leave the cauli to steam dry.

Meanwhile, cut the fennel into fine wedges, keeping the bases intact.

Add to the bowl with the cauli, pour in half of the olive oil and toss to coat. Transfer to a baking tray and place in the oven, close to the top.

Into the same oily bowl, pop the butter beans, garlic, fennel seeds, lemon peel and a pinch of salt flakes, then drizzle with the rest of the olive oil and toss about to coat. Transfer to a second baking tray. Nestle the feta block into the middle of the tray of beans.

Place towards the bottom of the oven, and leave both trays to roast for 20–25 minutes until the fennel and cauli have softened and coloured, and the feta has started to burnish and curl at the edges, swapping the trays halfway through if need be.

1 small cauliflower, about 1 kg (2 lb 2 oz), torn into small florets, stem sliced into small bites

2 small fennel bulbs (or 1 medium), fronds reserved

⅓ cup (80 ml) extra virgin olive oil, plus extra for finishing

2 x 400 g (14 oz) tins butter beans (lima beans)

2–3 garlic cloves, skin on

1 tablespoon fennel seeds

1 lemon, peeled and pith removed, juice reserved for the dressing

200 g (7 oz) block of creamy feta (such as Danish)

GOLDEN RAISIN DRESSING

½ cup (85 g) golden raisins (sultanas)

¼ cup (60 ml) extra virgin olive oil

½ teaspoon salt flakes

FINAL BITS & BOBS

⅓ cup (45 g) slivered almonds, toasted

1 tablespoon runny honey

To make the dressing, pour the reserved lemon juice over the golden raisins. When the trays come out of the oven, use tongs to collect the garlic and set aside to cool slightly. Squeeze out the pulp of the garlic cloves over the golden raisins, adding any residual pan juices and the olive oil and salt. Whisk together with a fork to combine, then taste and season with additional salt and pepper if need be. Discard garlic skins.

Put the veg, beans and feta into a mixing bowl and toss about gently to break the feta up.

When ready to serve, transfer the feta'd veg and beans to a serving platter. Shower the golden raisin dressing mixture over the lot. Scatter the slivered almonds on top and drizzle with honey, finishing with the reserved fennel fronds. Give it all one last crack of pepper, and a final flourish of extra olive oil.

FRIENDS WITH

Green veg moghrabieh with yoghurt drizzle p70

I like to think of this salad as Sunshine & Rainbows. Adding marmalade to the dressing is sunshine: sweetness and bitterness in equal measure, with a golden colour that radiates against the stark whiteness of the ricotta salata. This is ricotta that's been aged enough to harden, so you can shave it with a peeler or mandolin. You could also crumble it or finely grate it. If you can't find ricotta salata at your local deli, use blobs of fresh ricotta and an extra pinch of flaky salt. The rainbow chard quickle will last in the fridge for up to a month: use it as you would any pickle, for pops of acidity.

Carrot & wild rice salad *with* marmalade dressing

Bring a large saucepan of water to the boil with the bay leaves and garlic cloves. Tip in wild rice, bring back to the boil, then drop to a gentle burble and cook for 45 minutes or until tender.

Meanwhile, slice the carrots in half lengthways and toss together with 2 tablespoons of the olive oil, the caraway seeds and some salt and pepper. Spread on baking paper in a shallow roasting tin and pop into the oven, then crank to 200°C (400°F) or 180°C (350°F) fan forced and roast for 25 minutes or so until tender, tossing halfway through (these cook better if started off in a cold oven).

To make the quickled rainbow stems, combine vinegar, ½ cup (125 ml) of water, the sugar and salt in a small saucepan and bring to a gentle boil on low to medium heat. Drop to a gentle simmer for a few minutes.

Slice the chard stems into 1 cm (⅜ inch) half-moons, splitting any thicker stems in half. Place in a clean glass jar or heatproof container with the spices and orange peel. Pour the hot pickling liquor over and set aside to cool.

When rice is tender, drain well, discard the bay leaves, but keep the garlic cloves. Return to the pot along with the chard leaves, a pinch of salt flakes and a glug of olive oil. Fluff together with a fork, breaking up the softened garlic, then pop the lid on and leave to steam dry for 10 minutes.

Make the marmalade dressing by heating the ingredients in a small saucepan, then gently simmering it uncovered for 5 minutes. Take it off the heat and reserve.

When the carrots come out of the oven, pour the dressing over the carrots in the roasting tin, stirring about to combine with all of the pan juices.

Tip the wild rice mixture onto a platter, then top with the dressed sunshine carrots and all of the pan juices. Garnish with quickled rainbow stems, parsley and shaved ricotta salata.

2–3 bay leaves

2–3 garlic cloves, bruised and peeled

1 cup (200 g) wild rice, washed

2 bunches Dutch carrots, scrubbed

¼ cup (60 ml) extra virgin olive oil, plus extra for finishing

1 teaspoon caraway seeds, crushed slightly

1 bunch rainbow chard, stems trimmed and reserved for pickling, leaves torn

QUICKLED RAINBOW STEMS

½ cup (125 ml) white wine or apple cider vinegar

1 teaspoon sugar

1 tablespoon salt flakes

1 teaspoon caraway seeds

4 peppercorns

1 bay leaf

1 slice orange peel

MARMALADE DRESSING

¼ cup (60 ml) extra virgin olive oil

Zest and juice of 1 orange

1 thumb ginger, finely grated

1 small garlic clove, finely grated

1 tablespoon orange marmalade

¼ cup (40 g) currants

1 teaspoon salt flakes

¼ teaspoon freshly cracked black pepper

FINAL BITS & BOBS

¼ cup loosely packed parsley leaves, roughly chopped

50 g (1¾ oz) ricotta salata

FRIENDS WITH

Hot pink pear salad with zippy kale and ricotta p188

Parsnips become so sweet when roasted, and the creaminess of the whipped tarator is perfectly cut through by the gentle gingery hum of heat in the herbaceous chermoula! Tarator and chermoula are Levantine gifts, and remind me of touring with Yotam Ottolenghi. For a whole fortnight, we'd cap off our shows across Australia and New Zealand with a cook-off, and one of the options was chermoula – almost always a winning element. The aquafaba from the chickpeas behaves like egg white and will fluff up the tarator. If you want to bulk out this dish for a crowd, use two tins of chickpeas.

Roasted parsnip salad *with* almond tarator *and* chermoula

Spread blanched almonds on a large baking tray and have a second tray handy too. Preheat the oven to 200°C (400°F) or 180°C (350°F) fan forced with both baking trays inside, checking on the almonds after 10 minutes. Transfer the almonds to a small bowl and set aside until needed.

Carefully line both of the preheated baking trays with baking paper.

Peel the parsnips and cut them into 1 cm x 5 cm (⅜ inch x 2 inch) batons. Core the pears and slice into wedges.

In a large bowl, toss the parsnip, pear, onion, olives and chickpeas with the olive oil and za'atar (if the za'atar is unsalted, add a pinch of salt flakes) then tumble onto the two trays. Roast for about 35–40 minutes until the parsnips are starting to soften and scorch and the chickpeas are golden and crispy.

Meanwhile, to make the whipped almond tarator, put ¾ cup (120 g) of the reserved toasted almonds (save the remainder for garnish), garlic, tahini, olive oil, lemon zest and juice, salt and pepper into a blender with ½ cup (125 ml) of the reserved aquafaba. Blitz to a fluffy 'whipped' consistency, taste and season with salt and pepper. Add more aquafaba and blitz again if more lightness is needed.

To make the chermoula, reserve a few of the parsley and coriander leaves for a garnish. Put remaining ingredients in a small blender and blitz until super smooth.

When parsnips are done, scoop the tarator onto a shallow platter and layer the roasted parsnip, onion, pear, olives and chickpeas over, then dress with the chermoula and top with the reserved toasted almonds, pear matchsticks, reserved parsley and coriander leaves, and one last glug of extra olive oil.

Serve warm or at room temperature.

1 cup (160 g) blanched almonds

600 g (1 lb 5 oz) parsnips

2 pears, such as beurre bosc or packham

2 red onions, cut into wedges

½ cup (100 g) large green pitted olives

400 g (14 oz) chickpeas, drained and rinsed (aquafaba reserved for tarator)

¼ cup (60 ml) extra virgin olive oil, plus extra for drizzling

2 tablespoons za'atar

WHIPPED ALMOND TARATOR

1 garlic clove

2 tablespoons tahini

½ cup (125 ml) extra virgin olive oil

Zest and juice of 1 lemon

½ teaspoon salt flakes

¼ teaspoon freshly ground pepper

CHERMOULA DRESSING

¼ cup loosely packed parsley leaves

¼ cup coriander (cilantro) leaves

1 garlic clove

1 tablespoon runny honey

1 preserved lemon cheek, pith and flesh removed

1 thumb ginger, coarsely chopped

¼ cup (60 ml) extra virgin olive oil

Zest and juice of 1 lemon

FINAL BITS & BOBS

1 firm pear, such as beurre bosc or packham, cored and cut into matchsticks

FRIENDS WITH

Silverbeet & broccoli tumble with herby avocado dressing p220

These are the things you'd expect to see in a slaw, but hot. The juniper dressing is like serving a gin and tonic with your roast veg, and yes, this means you can also use this with leftover veggies from last night's dinner. Juniper berries are STRONG – you don't need much to make this jump! See how the purple cabbage keeps its shape and colour? That's because the heat's high enough to burnish without leaching anthocyanin into the pan. Some veg is more leaky than others, so we're mitigating intermingling of colours with separate roasting trays. If you can't find Dutchies, use regular carrots.

Warm winter slaw *with* honey & juniper dressing

Preheat the oven to 200°C (400°F) or 180°C (350°F) fan forced. Line 2 baking trays with baking paper. Pop the wedges of cabbage and red onion on one tray and the carrots and fennel wedges on the other, then brush the vegetables with olive oil, sprinkling the lot with fennel seeds, salt and pepper.

Whack the trays into the oven and roast for 45 minutes, or until the vegies start to caramelise and the tips of the onion and cabbage wedges are starting to curl.

Meanwhile, make the honey and juniper dressing by simply whisking everything together.

When everything in the oven has capitulated to the wonders of quality time under heat, tumble them into the salad bowl and pour the whisked dressing over. Sprinkle with the chives, reserved parsley and fennel fronds, and finish with a flourish of olive oil, salt flakes and freshly cracked pepper. Serve immediately while hot or at room temperature.

½ red cabbage, cut into 8 wedges

1 red onion, halved and cut into wedges

1 bunch Dutch carrots, trimmed and scrubbed, larger carrots halved

1 small fennel bulb, about 200 g (7 oz), trimmed and cut into wedges, fronds reserved for garnish

¼ cup (60 ml) extra virgin olive oil, plus extra for finishing

1 teaspoon fennel seeds

1 teaspoon salt

¼ teaspoon finely cracked black pepper

HONEY & JUNIPER DRESSING

1 tablespoon runny honey

2 tablespoons apple cider vinegar

1 tablespoon dijon mustard

2 dried juniper berries, finely chopped or crushed

1 garlic clove, minced

¼ cup (60 ml) extra virgin olive oil

½ teaspoon salt flakes

2 tablespoons finely chopped parsley stems, leaves picked and reserved for garnish

FINAL BITS & BOBS

2 tablespoons finely chopped chives

FRIENDS WITH

Yampers (camper's jacket yams) p160

Cauliflower's mildness means it happily soaks up whatever flavours you fancy. The more you throw at it, the more interesting it becomes. Applying heat brings out its salted caramel sweetness; pickling, its juicy crunch. The cauli takes on colour very easily, too, which is why a few wedges of beetroot turn this pickle into glittering garnets like jewels in the crown. Once you get the hang of hot-pickling, make your own turnips for shawarma or daikon batons for salady crunch. You'll find cracked burghul in the health food aisle or bulk wholefood stores, or to go gluten-free use brown rice, puy lentils or quinoa instead. Make this salad fully plant-based by holding off on the yoghurt in the dressing and subbing in almond feta or another kind of creamy nut cheese. You can buy pomegranate seeds, or just cut a pomegranate in half and smack its bottom with a wooden spoon over a bowl and watch the garnet gems fly out. For larger poms, I like to lop just a little off the top, expose the membrane points, then slice and open it up to a star, or pop out segment by segment. You can keep leftover seeds on damp paper towel in the fridge to use in other dishes.

Cypriot salad *with* pink pickled cauliflower

To make the pink pickled cauliflower, put 3 cups (750 ml) of water into a large saucepan with the vinegar, sugar and spices and bring to a steady boil. Chop one half of the cauli into small florets, place in a heatproof bowl with the beetroot and bay leaves, then carefully pour the boiling pickling liquid over the veg to cover, making sure all of the vegetables are submerged by placing a clean saucer on top. Leave on the bench to cool and soak up the pink hue. This can be done a day in advance, or longer, if you pickle into sterilised jars.

Preheat the oven to 200°C (400°F) or 180°C (350°F) fan forced. Line a large baking tray with baking paper and spread the nut and seed mix on the tray. Pop it in the oven, setting the timer for 10 minutes. Check the nuts and seeds, giving them a shimmy if they need a little longer to colour, or pulling them out at this point. Transfer to a small heatproof bowl and set aside to cool, keeping the lined tray for the cauli to come.

Break the remaining cauliflower half into small florets, trim the stalk and cut into small fork-sized chunks. Put the cauliflower in a bowl with chickpeas, onion, olive oil, cumin seeds, salt and pepper and toss to coat.

Scatter the bowl of cauli and bits over the baking tray and roast for 30 minutes or until the cauliflower is golden and onion is softened and gnarly on the tips.

1 cauliflower, halved

1 cup mixed nuts and seeds (such as almonds, pistachios, pepitas and sunflower seeds) roughly chopped

400 g (14 oz) tin chickpeas, drained and rinsed

1 red onion, sliced into 1 cm (⅜ inch) wedges

¼ cup (60 ml) extra virgin olive oil, plus extra to drizzle the burghul

2 teaspoons cumin seeds

½ teaspoon sea salt flakes

½ teaspoon cracked black pepper

⅔ cup (125 g) fine burghul

200 ml (7 fl oz) boiling water

½ cup roughly chopped parsley leaves

½ cup roughly chopped mint leaves

Seeds of 1 pomegranate

PINK PICKLED CAULIFLOWER

1 cup (250 ml) white wine vinegar

¼ cup (55 g) sugar

1 teaspoon cumin seeds

1 tablespoon salt flakes

1 tablespoon peppercorns

1 large beetroot (beet), peeled and chopped into thin wedges

3 bay leaves

GARLICKY YOGHURT DRESSING

½ cup (125 ml) extra virgin olive oil

3 heaped tablespoons Greek yoghurt

1 tablespoon lemon juice

1 teaspoon white wine vinegar

2–3 garlic cloves

2 teaspoons runny honey

1 teaspoon sea salt flakes

While the cauli mix is roasting, pop the burghul in a large heatproof bowl, pour the boiling water over it and cover with a plate. Set aside to soak for 10 minutes, then drizzle with extra olive oil and fluff with a fork.

To make the garlicky yoghurt dressing, put all of the ingredients together in a blender and whizz to emulsify. Check for stray chunks of garlic, scrape down the side, and give it another blitz.

When ready to serve, toss the burghul, nuts and seeds, herbs and half the dressing together in a bowl, then arrange on a serving platter or in a shallow salad bowl. Tumble the roasted cauli mix over, as well as the pickled cauli and pomegranate seeds. Drizzle with the remaining dressing to serve.

FRIENDS WITH

Pumpkin wedges with toasty seeds and dill tahini p168

I can't tell you how great this salad is for kids, and those young at heart – like a school-camp baked potato, made salady. You could certainly do this with potatoes, but I like the way sweet potato or yam brings another level of lovely caramelness and colour. Using tinned corn is more authentically campy, but if you have fresh cobs, boil for 4 minutes, then shave off the kernels. Ghanaian chef Selassie Atadika taught me that sweet potato leaves are used like spinach in her neck of the woods, so if that's yours too, feel free to double down on sweet potato from root to leaf. Complete the campfire effect with smoked salt if it's already in your pantry. If using a big sweet potato or yam, roast it whole (which'll take about an hour) or chop it into chunky bits to shorten the cooking time.

Yampers (camper's jacket yams)

Pop sweet potatoes onto a lined tray and into a cold oven. Crank the heat to 220°C (430°F) or 200°C (400°F) fan forced, then roast them nudey rudey (undressed) for 40 minutes, until they blister, burst and yield to the touch.

Make the sour cream and chive drizzle by whisking the ingredients together, tasting and seasoning with more salt and pepper if needed.

Toss together shredded cabbage, carrot, vinegar and salt, then season to taste with more salt and a generous crack of pepper.

To assemble, lay a bed of baby spinach in the base of a large shallow bowl, then arrange the baked sweet potatoes, still in their jackets, over the top. Pierce into each with whatever implement is to hand by criss-crossing, then squashing down a little to expose the vibrant orange (or purple!) innards. Sprinkle the cheddar cheese over the innards while still warm, to let the cheese melt.

Pour half of the sour cream and chive drizzle over the top in broad strokes, then tumble on the cabbage and carrot slaw and the cooked corn. Finish off with more of the drizzle over the top, then sprinkle with extra chives and drizzle with the extra virgin olive oil. Crack pepper on and call it a day.

6–8 small sweet potatoes, about 1 kg (2 lb 4 oz), washed

100 g (3½ oz) red cabbage, finely shredded

1 carrot, about 100 g (3½ oz), finely shredded

2 teaspoons apple cider vinegar

1 teaspoon salt flakes

SOUR CREAM & CHIVE DRIZZLE

100 g (3½ oz) sour cream

50 g (1¾ oz) pouring cream

2 teaspoons apple cider vinegar

2 teaspoons dijon mustard

2 tablespoons finely chopped chives, plus extra for garnish

½ teaspoon salt flakes

¼ teaspoon freshly cracked black pepper

FINAL BITS & BOBS

50 g (1¾ oz) baby spinach leaves

80 g (2¾ oz) cheddar cheese, grated

1 cup (200 g) corn kernels

2 tablespoons extra virgin olive oil

FRIENDS WITH

Warm winter slaw with honey & juniper dressing p154

You know those salad-bar salads at the airport or shopping centre, where it's just pasta underneath a catfish layer of pumpkin? That's because it hasn't been properly tossed. In this bowl, you won't be digging into nothing, you'll be mining pure gold. Because it's such brill bowl food – like a slippery risoni that's great hot or cold – it makes a lovely lunch *al desko* for big meeting days, when you're not sure if you'll get to eat. There's no need to peel the squash, as the skin softens in the oven. If you've got macadamia oil, use it to finish this. If you don't have macadamias, use blanched almonds.

Honeyed butternut risoni salad *with* marinated feta

800 g (1 lb 12 oz) butternut pumpkin (squash)

⅓ cup (80 ml) extra virgin olive oil

⅛ teaspoon ground cinnamon

1 tablespoon runny honey

1 cup (125 g) raw macadamias

1 cup (220 g) risoni

100 g (3½ oz) baby rocket (arugula)

CARAMELISED LEEK DRESSING

2 large leeks, finely sliced

2 tablespoons extra virgin olive oil

1 garlic clove, bruised

¼ cup (60 ml) apple cider vinegar

2 tablespoons runny honey

FINAL BITS & BOBS

100 g (3½ oz) marinated feta

Preheat the oven to 200°C (400°F) or 180°C (350°F) fan forced. Line 2 large baking trays with baking paper.

To caramelise the leeks for the dressing, toss the slices in the olive oil, then transfer to one of the baking trays and roast on a lower shelf for 15–20 minutes until soft and starting to brown on the edges.

Meanwhile, cut the butternut pumpkin into 1 cm (⅜ inch) cubes. Toss the cubes with ¼ cup (60 ml) of the olive oil, the cinnamon and a good pinch of salt and freshly cracked pepper and spread over the other baking tray, then whack into the oven to cook for 20 minutes on a high shelf. When browned and softened, drizzle with the honey and scatter with the macadamias and pop back in the oven for 5–10 minutes until macadamias have coloured up to a golden brown. Set aside to cool.

Cook the risoni according to packet instructions, drain well and toss with the remaining tablespoon of olive oil. Spread out on a shallow tray to cool and dry out a little without clumping.

To make the caramelised leek dressing, rub a medium heatproof bowl with the bruised garlic, then pour in the apple cider vinegar and the honey and stir together. Scoop the caramelised leeks into the bowl along with all of their pan juices, stirring about to combine. Taste and season with salt and pepper, and if you feel like it could use a kick, crush in the garlic (or sprinkle in a little garlic powder).

Toss the cooled risoni with the dressing, rocket, pumpkin and macadamias, then top with feta.

FRIENDS WITH

Frisée, witlof & grilled fig with goat's cheese p136

Here's a terrific salad that shifts with the seasons. You can make it warm, with frozen broad beans in autumn and winter, or mark the beginnings of spring with fresh broadies and a cooled cauli mix instead. Miso marinade like this often gets used on firm fish such as cod, or on chicken bits for grilling (cauli *is* the chicken of the soil!). Use the miso type you like the most or already have in the fridge, though I tend to think that milder white (shiro) miso works best here if you're investing.

Miso-roasted cauli
with broad bean smash

For the broad bean smash, turn the oven on to 220°C (430°F) or 200°C (400°F) fan forced. Line a baking tray with baking paper. Pop the blanched almonds onto the tray and into the oven as it's heating. Set the timer for 10 minutes and pull them out when they're golden (ovens vary in how quickly they heat up, so keep an eye out).

Bring a large saucepan of well-salted water to the boil.

While the water's coming to the boil, make the miso marinade by combining the olive oil, miso, tahini and garlic in a medium heatproof bowl. Taste and season with salt and pepper.

Pop the cauliflower florets into the boiling water for 4 minutes until they just become translucent. Use a slotted spoon to scoop the florets straight from the water into the bowl of miso marinade, draining well as you go. Leave the florets to soak up the flavours for 10 minutes or so. Keep the water boiling for the broad beans.

Pop the broad beans into the still-boiling water for 3–4 minutes. Once they're cooked, pull them out and run them under the tap to cool. Reserve a third of the broad beans for the smash, then double-pod the rest.

Separate the watercress leaves from the stems and pop the leaves into chilled water and back into the fridge if you've got space.

1 small cauliflower, about 1 kg (2 lb 4 oz), torn into small florets

500 g (1 lb 2 oz) podded broad beans

1 bunch watercress, about 200g (7 oz)

MISO MARINADE

¼ cup (60 ml) extra virgin olive oil

2 tablespoons shiro (white) miso paste

1 tablespoon tahini

1 garlic clove, minced

BROAD BEAN SMASH

½ cup (80 g) blanched almonds

½ bunch mint, about 20 g (¾ oz), keeping the tender mint tips for garnish

2 garlic cloves

1 cup (250 ml) extra virgin olive oil, plus extra for finishing

Zest and juice of 1 lemon

1 tablespoon shiro (white) miso paste, plus extra if needed

1 tablespoon tahini

1 teaspoon salt flakes

¼ teaspoon freshly cracked black pepper

Spread the marinated cauliflower onto the baking tray and squash the florets down with something heavy, such as an olive oil bottle or by applying some pressure through the back of a spoon, until they're splayed. Pop the tray into the oven for 15–20 minutes until the florets are crispy and golden. Reserve the residual liquid in the bottom of the miso marinade bowl for the smash.

To make the smash, put the reserved broad beans into a food processor with the mint leaves and stems (discarding any super woody ones) and watercress stems. Add the toasted almonds. Blitz, along with the garlic, olive oil, lemon zest and juice, miso and tahini, until smooth. Season with the salt and pepper, adding more miso if needed, and thin down with some of the reserved miso marinade liquid.

When ready to serve, toss the roasted cauliflower through the smash and pour onto a large platter. Top with the reserved watercress leaves, podded broad beans and reserved mint tips. Finish with a flourish of extra virgin olive oil, a crack of pep and a twinkle of salt flakes.

FRIENDS WITH

Skordalia with asparagus and potato peel crisps p96, Broccoli and cashew salad-fry p216

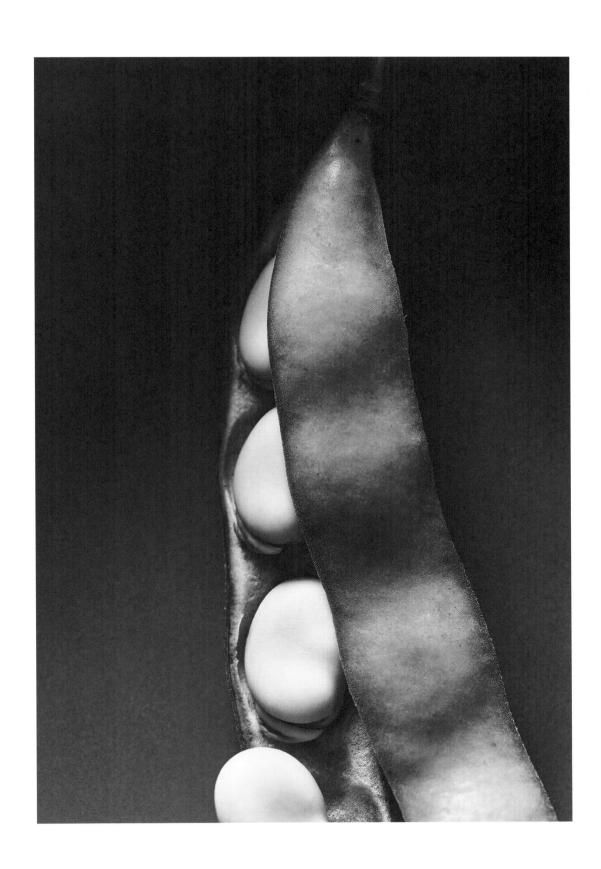

Pumpkin's a happy hero for any vego guests; it loves being treated like a big hunk of meat by being roasted until burnished and softened through the middle. You could also make a real meal out of this for all eaters by grilling some lamb koftas to peek out from around the pumpkin sails or to serve on the side. Think of them more like an accompaniment to the pumpkin than the other way around. Zhuzh it up with something saucy like this refreshing dill tahini yoghurt, and finish with the crunch of seeds for bonus texture. Sub out natural yoghurt for coconut yoghurt to make it fully plant-based.

Pumpkin wedges *with* toasty seeds *and* dill tahini

Preheat the oven to 220°C (430°F) or 200°C (400°F) fan forced, with your pumpkin roasting tray inside, scattered with the pepitas and sesame seeds. Set a timer for 10 minutes and pull the seeds out once they have reached their terrifically toasty potential. Transfer to a bowl and set aside until serving.

Wash pumpkin well (no need to peel) and slice into 4 cm (1½ inch) thick half-moons. Coat the pumpkin in olive oil, arrange tips-up on the preheated tray so that the pumpkin bits stand proud like sails in the oven, then roast for 45–50 minutes until soft through the centre.

Meanwhile, blitz the dill tahini yoghurt ingredients in a blender or food processor until combined. If making the dressing the old-fashioned way (unplugged), mince the garlic and finely chop the dill stalks then stir the rest of the ingredients together until uniformly green.

To serve, slather half of the dill tahini yoghurt on the bottom of a serving platter or board, arrange pumpkin on top, then drizzle on the rest of the dressing and scatter with toasted seeds, pomegranate seeds, reserved dill fronds and mint leaves. Finish with a final bedrizzle of extra olive oil and serve with lemon for squeezing over.

2 tablespoons pepitas (pumpkin seeds)

2 tablespoons sesame seeds

1 kg (2 lb 4 oz) jap, kabocha or kent pumpkin (squash)

2 tablespoons extra virgin olive oil, plus extra for drizzling

DILL TAHINI YOGHURT

2–3 garlic cloves

½ cup firmly packed dill, plus ¼ cup of extra fronds for garnish

½ cup (130 g) natural yoghurt

¼ cup (60 ml) tahini

Zest and juice of 1 lemon

2 teaspoons pomegranate molasses

1 teaspoon salt flakes

¼ teaspoon freshly cracked black pepper

FINAL BITS & BOBS

Seeds of half a pomegranate

Small mint leaves

1 lemon, halved

FRIENDS WITH

Cypriot salad with pink pickled cauliflower p156, Orange veg on green'd quinoa p170

What makes this such a great brunch salad is that it's full of colour (not just orange) and gut-loving ingredients that will make you zing, AND it's easy to batch-cook the elements ahead and assemble at the last minute like you've opened a cafe in your house (that might just serve better food than the one down the road). If you like a good hit of fire, feel free to sploosh the lot with plenty of hot sauce. The paprika'd veg already tastes a bit bacony, but you're welcome to add bacon as well if you're that way inclined. Equally, you could add an extra tin of black beans or chickpeas to make it even more filling. Use whatever light-coloured vinegar you've got for poaching the eggs, or even a lemon's worth of juice. Like any legume, quinoa always benefits from a soak to neutralise its protective outer coating for better digestion. Two hours should do it, but overnight is best.

Orange veg *on* green'd quinoa

Preheat the oven to 210°C (410°F) or 190°C (375°F) fan forced, with 2 baking trays inside, and the pepitas scattered on the top tray. Set the timer for 10 minutes and pull the pepitas out. Transfer to a bowl and set aside until serving.

Meanwhile, prep the orange veg. If the butternut comes complete with seeds, scoop these out. Cut the butternut into 2 cm (¾ inch) cubes, keeping the skin on. Cut the carrots into 2 cm (¾ inch) pieces, trying to keep the pieces roughly the same size. Toss into a large bowl and dress with the olive oil, maple syrup and paprika, and season with a pinch of salt flakes and freshly ground pepper.

When the oven is at temperature, carefully line the hot trays with baking paper, then arrange your veg on the trays. Roast the carrots and butternut pumpkin for 40–45 minutes until softened, golden and slightly blistered.

Drain the quinoa and give it a good rinse. Pop into a medium saucepan with 1½ cups (375 ml) of water, bring to the boil, then cover and simmer for about 15 minutes. Turn off the heat and leave to steam for 10 minutes with the lid on.

To make the coriander chimichurri, blitz together all of the ingredients in a food processor or muddle about in a mortar and pestle to a deep green paste. Taste and season if needed.

50 g (1¾ oz) pepitas (pumpkin seeds)

½ butternut pumpkin (squash), about 500 g (1 lb 2 oz)

2 large carrots

⅓ cup (80 ml) extra virgin olive oil

2 tablespoons maple syrup

½ teaspoon smoked paprika

1 cup (200 g) tricolour quinoa, soaked

1 tablespoon white vinegar

4 eggs

120 g (4½ oz) tin black beans, drained and rinsed

CORIANDER CHIMICHURRI

¼ cup (60 ml) extra virgin olive oil

2 tablespoons red wine vinegar

2 teaspoons maple syrup

½ red onion, coarsely chopped

4 garlic cloves

1 bunch parsley, coarsely chopped, pretty leaves reserved for garnish

1 bunch coriander (cilantro), pretty leaves reserved for garnish

1 teaspoon salt flakes

¼ teaspoon freshly cracked black pepper

FINAL BITS & BOBS

200 g (7 oz) haloumi, patted dry and
    sliced into batons

Olive oil, for frying and drizzling

2 avocados

Juice of 1 lime

40 g (1½ oz) red sauerkraut

To poach the eggs, bring a medium saucepan of well-salted water to the boil, and splash in the vinegar. When the water is at a boil, drop the heat to a simmer, crack each egg onto a small saucer, and gently tip it into the water from as close to the simmering water as possible. Set a timer for 2 minutes for very runny, or 3 minutes for firmer. Scoop out, drain on paper towel, and reserve.

Fluff up the quinoa with a fork, then toss half of the chimichurri and the black beans through the warm quinoa and pop the lid back on.

Just before you're ready to serve, heat a non-stick frying pan to smoking. Toss the haloumi batons in oil, then char until coloured. Slice the avocado finely and squeeze a little lime juice over the top.

Transfer the greened quinoa and beans to a serving platter, then tumble the orange veg on top, along with the rest of the chimichurri, the sauerkraut, haloumi and avocado. Finish with the pretty leaves, a drizzle of olive oil and the toasted pepitas.

FRIENDS WITH

Devilled egg and baby spinach salad p200

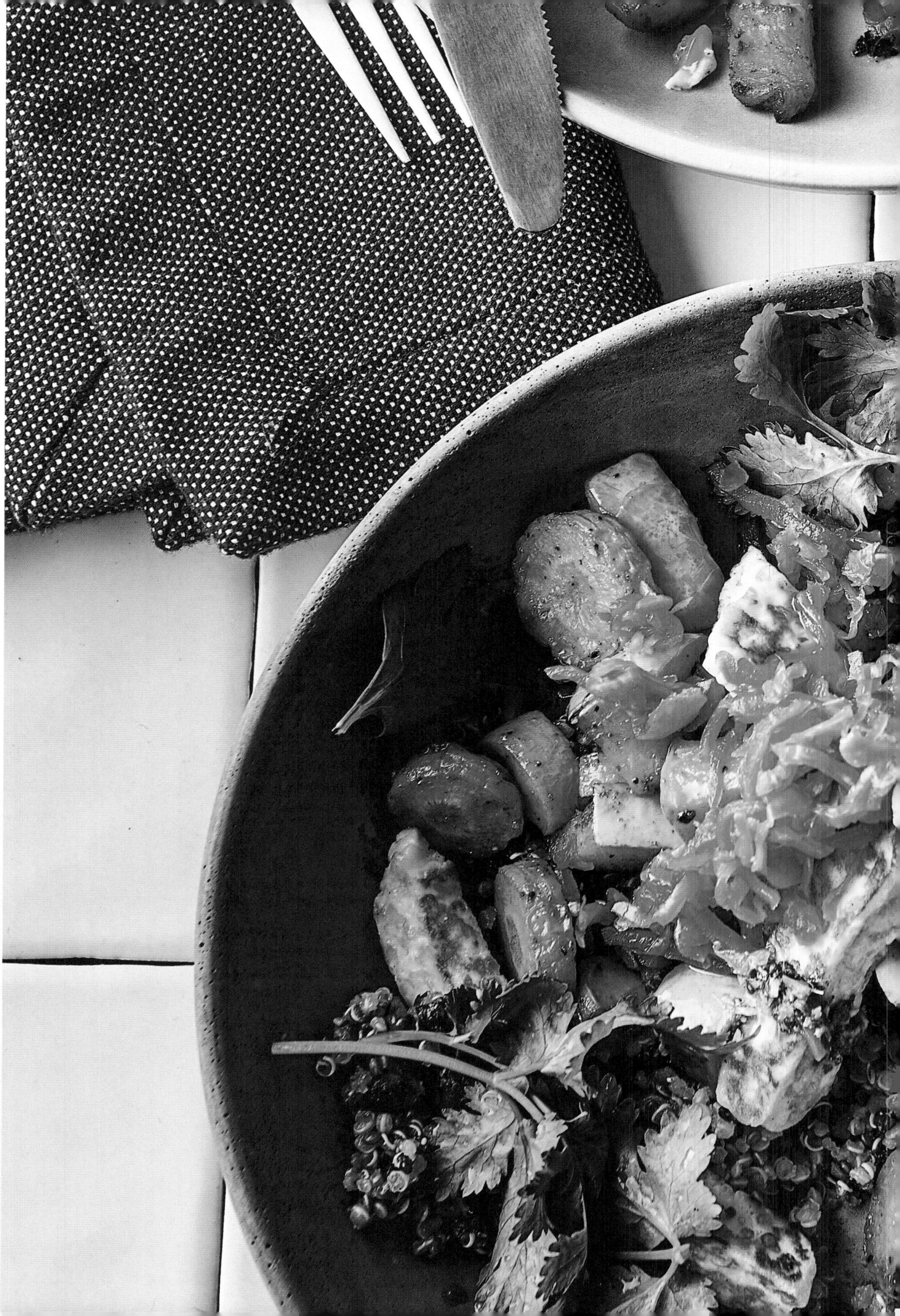

This dressing is actually a riff on a New Orleans classic sandwich: the muffuletta. Traditionally, it's served with plenty of deli meats such as sopressa, mortadella and coppa inside a rustic yeasted loaf, but we've swapped the salumi for slippery peppers in traffic light hues. Different coloured capsicums have varying levels of sweetness, bitterness and piquancy, and combining them is a bit like the Gibb brothers (aka the Bee Gees) – in perfect sibling harmony. Not making this would be a ... TRAGEDY!

Tricolour piperade *with* muffuletta dressing

In a large heavy-bottomed saucepan with a lid, sweat the onion in the olive oil for 8–10 minutes until softened, then lift the lid and let the onion start to singe at the edges. Using a slotted spoon, transfer the singed onion to a large bowl and reserve, leaving the oil in the pan.

Add the capsicum slices to the oil in the pan, toss around and sauté for 5 minutes until just heated through. Using a slotted spoon, transfer the capsicum to the bowl with the onion, leaving as much of the oil and juice as possible in the pan.

To make the muffuletta dressing, heat the strained oily capsicum liquor in the pan on low to medium heat, adding the olive oil, garlic and paprika. Gently heat for a couple of minutes. Plonk in the chopped olives, pickled vegetables and capers. Heat through, then pour in the red wine vinegar. Take off the heat and stir in the herbs and provolone, then season with freshly ground black pepper.

Toss the hot dressing with the warm peppers and onion, transfer to a serving platter and pour over the residual dressing. Finish with a drizzle of extra virgin olive oil.

1 red onion, finely sliced with the grain

¼ cup (60 ml) extra virgin olive oil, plus extra for drizzling

4 large mixed coloured capsicums (peppers), about 1 kg (2 lb 4 oz), finely sliced with the vertical curve

MUFFULETTA DRESSING

2 tablespoons extra virgin olive oil

4 garlic cloves, finely sliced

½ teaspoon sweet paprika

¼ cup (50 g) stuffed green olives, finely chopped

¼ cup (50 g) pitted kalamata olives, finely chopped

¼ cup (50 g) giardiniera (pickled vegetables), finely chopped

1 tablespoon brined capers

2 tablespoons red wine vinegar

1 tablespoon finely chopped tarragon leaves

2 tablespoons finely chopped parsley leaves

100 g (3½ oz) provolone cheese, cubed

FRIENDS WITH

Calamari and shell pasta salad p133

Persian feta is a shapeshifter, capable of remaining firm and steadfast when crumbled across the top of a platter or salad, or of yielding to a soft, velvety cream to enhance all manner of dishes from pasta to pesto to papula, a creamy Balkan bean dip. Here, I've utilised it in both capacities, first as a bodybuilder for the creamy, funky schmear, then dotted along the top to add texture and pops of bright white against the crimson of the capsicum. Putting the garlic inside the capsicum while roasting flavours it and keeps the garlic from burning. Serving with crusty bread is a crowd cracker.

Charred capsicum *on* feta & butterbean purée

6 red capsicums (peppers)

4 garlic cloves, unpeeled

2 tablespoons extra virgin olive oil

FETA & BUTTERBEAN PURÉE

275 g (9¾ oz) jar marinated Persian feta, drained, oil and aromatics reserved

400 g (14 oz) tin butter beans (lima beans), drained but not rinsed

1 tablespoon sherry vinegar

¼ cup (60 ml) extra virgin olive oil, plus extra for drizzling

1 garlic clove

1 teaspoon salt flakes, plus extra for sprinkling

FINAL BITS & BOBS

Small Turkish pide

2 tablespoons finely chopped parsley leaves

¼ teaspoon sweet paprika (optional but excellent)

¼ cup (40 g) roasted almonds, roughly chopped

Preheat the oven to 220°C (430°F) or 200°C (400°F) fan forced. Line a shallow roasting tin with baking paper.

Slice the tops off the capsicums and twist out the seedy centres and pithy membranes.

In a bowl, toss the capsicums and garlic cloves with the oil. Arrange the capsicum cut-side down in the roasting tin, popping a garlic clove under some of the capsicums, like little gnomes in their houses.

Roast for 35–40 minutes until capsicums are blistered and burnished and the garlic is buttery inside.

Meanwhile, reserve a good spoonful of feta for the garnish. Put the rest of the feta and residual aromatics from the feta jar, fishing out any peppercorns and bay leaves, into a blender with the drained butter beans, sherry vinegar, olive oil, garlic clove and salt flakes. Blitz until smooth and whipped.

Once the roasted garlic is cool enough to touch, squish the flesh out into the mixture and blitz again to combine. Taste and season with salt and pepper.

To easily remove the skins from the capsicums, cover with foil, or a second (inverted) baking tray, then leave for 15 minutes to steam. Once cool enough to handle, slip the skins off, then slice cheeks into thin slivers.

Pop the pide on a tray and into the still-hot oven to warm through.

To serve, scoop the feta and butterbean purée onto a large platter in undulating waves. Arrange capsicum slices on top in bright red glossy strips. Dress with the pan juices, sprinkle with parsley, paprika, almonds, extra olive oil and a pinch of salt flakes. Finish with a flourish of reserved feta. Pop pide nearby and encourage guests to scoop and dip to their heart's content.

FRIENDS WITH

Broccolini with self-saucing chickpeas p219

Cauliflower's sculpturesque otherworldliness loves to be oiled up and roasted whole. Like a chicken, cauli benefits from a baste in the oven every now and then for an extra-golden crust. Eyal Shani, the Israeli chef widely credited with bringing whole-roasting mainstream, recommends par-steaming the cauli for 10–15 minutes, then letting it cool, but I'm making it even easier by scalding the cauli instead (which, incidentally, is also my favourite way of preparing a chook before making chicken soup). Once you get the hang of this method, feel free to have a play with the aromatics you team it with: add North African spice mixes such as harissa into the base for a twist, or use burghul or freekeh underneath. If you prefer to keep your hands tidy, use gloves for massaging in the coconut–turmeric paste. You can also use half a jar of ready-made korma paste and just add the coconut cream. The colours are phenomenal, so this is best brought to the table whole and then handed over for your guest of honour to crack into. Like all good curries, this salad is still fantastic the next day.

Cauli korma crown
and cardamom brown rice

Preheat oven to 220°C (430°F) or 200°C (400°F) fan forced.

Put cauliflower stem-side down into a large bowl. Pour over boiling water to half-way up the side of the cauli and cover loosely. Set aside for 10 minutes.

To make the korma paste, combine all of the ingredients in a small bowl and mix well.

Drain cauliflower and place on top of the sliced onions in a snug, high-sided roasting dish (I use a ceramic pie dish) and rub liberally with coconut oil and turmeric. Roast for 30 minutes, until the curd starts to brown and you see the surface starting to crisp up.

While that's happening, you've got time to cook your rice. Bring a medium saucepan of water to a rolling boil and add the cardamom pods. Wash the rice well, drain and add to the pot, stirring occasionally until it comes back to the boil (this will take about 5–7 minutes on medium-high heat). Once the rice starts boiling again, set the timer for 15 minutes.

Drain well, shaking the rice vigorously to expel any residual water. Put the rice back into the drained pot with the cashews (reserving a few for garnish), sultanas and a pinch of salt flakes and steam for 10 minutes with the lid on. Pick out the spices and fluff the rice with a fork like it's couscous.

1 cauliflower

1 large onion, cut into 1 cm (⅜ inch) rings

2 tablespoons coconut oil

1 teaspoon ground turmeric

KORMA PASTE

1 teaspoon onion powder

1 teaspoon garlic powder

1 thumb ginger, peeled and grated

2 teaspoons mild madras curry powder

1 teaspoon garam masala

1 tablespoon tomato paste

140 g (5 oz) coconut cream

2 teaspoons brown sugar

½ teaspoon salt flakes

Good crack of pepper

CARDAMOM RICE

4 cardamom pods

1 cup (200 g) brown basmati rice

100 g (3½ oz) roasted cashews

½ cup (85 g) sultanas (golden raisins)

RAITA DRESSING

½ cup (130 g) natural yoghurt

1 garlic clove, crushed

2 tablespoons lemon juice

2 mint sprigs, finely chopped

¼ bunch coriander (cilantro), stems finely chopped, leaves reserved for garnish

FINAL BITS & BOBS

1 long red chilli, finely diced

1 lemon, cut into wedges

At the half hour mark, pull the cauliflower out of the baking dish and remove the caramelised and collapsed onions. Set them aside until ready to serve. Nestle the cauliflower back in the dish and smother with the korma paste. Pop back into the oven and roast for another 20–25 minutes or until the paste is deep brown and the cauli is fork tender.

To make the raita dressing, mix yoghurt, garlic and lemon juice together in a small bowl. Fold in the chopped mint and coriander stems and set aside.

Serve the warm rice on a platter or wide shallow salad bowl, add the whole korma'd cauliflower and top with raita dressing, onions and any pan juices. Garnish with reserved coriander leaves and cashews, diced chilli and wedges of lemon. Break the cauliflower open over the rice at the table, toss it all about and serve.

FRIENDS WITH

Blanch 'n' toss beans p204

Sticky, sweet, textural, meaty and just happens to be vegan? Tick, tick, tick, tick! This bowl's gloriously glistening with eggplant that's fried until it yields to silky strips, sponging up the sticky teriyaki sauce. Speaking of sponges, that's exactly what tofu puffs are, and they get even juicier in the dressing overnight. Udon noodles are nifty because they're slippery and chunky, and you'll find fresh udon noodles in the chilled section at the shops. You'll get the best spring onion curls if you pop them into iced water, but slicing them chunky to fry with the rest of the mix is also an option. This is delicious cold and can be made a day ahead and brought back to room temperature to serve.

Sticky eggplant, tofu *and* noodle salad

Cut eggplant into 1 cm (⅜ inch) slices lengthways, then into chunky chips about 5 cm (2 inches) long, sprinkle with salt and set aside in a colander for 30 minutes.

While you wait for the eggplant to sweat, make the teriyaki sauce. Combine all of the ingredients in a small saucepan, bring to the boil and simmer for 5 minutes.

Cook the udon noodles according to packet instructions and toss with a couple of tablespoons of the warm sauce.

Squeeze the eggplant through the colander and pat dry with paper towel.

Heat 1 cm (⅜ inch) of neutral oil in a wok or heavy-based frying pan until shimmering, then cook the eggplant in batches until golden (watch out – it might spit a little) for about 6 minutes, adding more oil if needed.

Once all of the eggplant is cooked, use the residual oil in the pan to give the torn tofu puffs a new lease on life, tossing about for a minute or two to turn slightly more golden.

Transfer most of the frying oil out of the pan into a heatproof bowl, leaving a couple of tablespoons remaining. Crank the heat to medium and, when the oil is shimmering once more, toss the tofu puffs and cooked eggplant back into the pan along with the sauce, sizzling everything together for a minute or so to coat and become glossy.

When ready to serve, arrange the udon on a platter and tumble the eggplant and tofu puffs with the sauce over the noodles. For the final bedazzle, sprinkle with drained and spun spring onions curls, and toasted sesame seeds.

2 eggplants (aubergines), about 800 g (1 lb 12 oz)

2 teaspoons salt flakes

200 g (7 oz) fresh udon noodles

Neutral oil for shallow-frying (I like rice bran or grapeseed)

200 g (7 oz) tofu puffs, torn in half

STICKY TERIYAKI SAUCE

½ cup (125 ml) light soy sauce

½ cup (110 g) brown sugar

1 tablespoon rice wine vinegar

2 teaspoons finely grated ginger

1 teaspoon finely grated garlic

1 teaspoon sesame oil

FINAL BITS & BOBS

2 spring onions (scallions), finely sliced on the diagonal and soaked in cold water

2 tablespoons sesame seeds, toasted

FRIENDS WITH
SPC long green veg p210

DEVILLED EGG AND
BABY SPINACH
SALAD (PAGE 200)

POTATO CRACK
SALAD WITH
FETA CRUMBLE
(PAGE 199)

ROASTED BEETS WITH SPICED WALNUTS AND GEORGIAN GARO (PAGE 187)

BLANCH 'N' TOSS BEANS (PAGE 204)

This is like a salad version of pkhali, a chunky Georgian dip, but instead of blitzing the beets, they're roasted in red wine vin and pom molasses until they're gorgeously glossy (more is more here!). If you're in a hurry but keen on making this dish, toss vac-packed cooked beets through warmed vinegar and molasses. Garo is a form of Georgian pesto. The walnuts, used in both the garo and garnish, are marvellously meaty, with the khmeli suneli mix a spiced sensation for salad sprinkling.

Roasted beets *with* spiced walnuts & Georgian garo

2 bunches baby beetroot (beets), about 12, tops off

2 tablespoons extra virgin olive oil, plus extra for drizzling

2 tablespoons red wine vinegar

1 teaspoon pomegranate molasses

KHMELI SUNELI SPICED WALNUTS

1 tablespoon pomegranate molasses

1–2 tablespoons extra virgin olive oil

¼ teaspoon garlic powder

½ teaspoon ground coriander

1 teaspoon ground fenugreek

½ teaspoon mild madras curry powder

1 cup (100 g) fresh walnuts

½ teaspoon salt flakes

GARO (GEORGIAN PESTO)

¼ cup khmeli suneli spiced walnuts (see above)

½ cup coriander (cilantro) stems, leaves reserved for garnish

4 garlic cloves

¼ cup (60 ml) extra virgin olive oil

2 tablespoons red wine vinegar

FINAL BITS & BOBS

Seeds of 1 pomegranate

Prepare the beetroot by keeping the smallest whole, with tails and a little of the tops on, halving the medium ones and quartering the large ones, reserving the small leaves for garnish. Soak in a bowl of cold water for 15 minutes to de-grit while you preheat the oven to 200°C (400°F) or 180°C (350°F) fan forced.

Drain and plonk the beets in a mixing bowl with the olive oil, red wine vinegar, pomegranate molasses and a good pinch of salt flakes. Transfer to a baking tray, cover with foil and roast for 40 minutes. Remove the foil and cook for a further 20 minutes or until fork-tender and shrivelled.

Meanwhile, prepare the khmeli suneli spiced walnuts. In a medium bowl, combine pomegranate molasses, olive oil and garlic powder with the spices. Toss in the walnuts and salt flakes and stir about to coat, giving the spices a chance to stick to each nut. Transfer to a lined baking tray.

Whack the nut tray in under the beet tray, and roast for 12 minutes. Pull out the tray and use tongs to separate any clusters. When crispy and cooled, transfer to a small bowl and set aside.

To make the garo, pop ¼ cup of the cooling spiced walnuts into a food processor with the rest of the garo ingredients and blitz to a rough pesto-like consistency.

When ready to serve, spoon the garo into the base of a shallow serving bowl, smushing it about with the back of the spoon to coat loosely. Give the beets one last toss in the tray to coat in the residual juices for extra gloss, then tumble them into the bowl and scatter with the walnuts, pomegranate seeds, reserved coriander leaves and baby beet leaves. Finish with a final drizzle of extra olive oil, salt flakes and cracked pepper.

FRIENDS WITH

Braised flat beans with Svanetia-spiced walnuts p208

Rumour has it that 20 years ago the biggest wholesale account for global kale growers was Pizza Hut. The frilly leaves were used as salad bar roughage, like curly parsley at a butcher's. When people asked if it could be eaten, the answer was a resounding NO! As the pizza chain's fortunes waned, kale's ubiquity sky-rocketed – an illustration of the old adage: don't peak in high school. Kale's glow-up has meant that people know they can chip it and roast it, but did you know that giving kale a good rub is enough to release its robust structure into a softer salad leaf? Beetroot is a natural food dye, and transforms plain pear into Barbie. And this Barbie is zero-waste, using the poaching syrup to make a stupendous shrub for serving alongside the salad.

Hot pink pear salad *with* zippy kale *and* ricotta

Peel and halve the pears, scooping out the cores with a teaspoon. Peel the beetroot and slice into 1 cm (⅜ inch) wedges.

Make a light sugar syrup by putting the sugar, honey, vinegar and fennel seeds into a saucepan with 4 cups (1 litre) of water. Bring to the boil over medium heat, stirring occasionally to help the sugar dissolve. When the sugar syrup has come to the boil, add the pear and beetroot and turn the heat down to barely a simmer. Use a heatproof saucer or small plate to help keep the pear and beetroot from bobbing to the surface. Simmer gently for an hour, or until the pears are tender when pierced with a skewer. Turn off the heat, whack a lid on and leave to cool (preferably overnight) in the liquid. The longer you can leave it, the better for colour: this can be done up to 48 hours in advance.

Add the lemon zest to the salt flakes, rubbing between your fingers to make a lemon salt, and set aside. Squeeze one of the lemon halves into a medium bowl of cold water to acidulate. (The remaining lemon halves are used for the vinaigrette.) Finely slice the fennel vertically on a mandolin, retaining the shape as much as possible. Pop the slices into the bowl of acidulated water as you go.

Wash, drain and strip the kale from its stems and tear into small pieces, or finely slice if your household are slower to warm to kale. Pour the lemon salt and olive oil over the prepared kale and massage until the kale relaxes and changes to a darker colour.

2 firm pears, such as packham or beurre bosc

2 small to medium beetroot (beets), about 400 g (14 oz)

1 cup (220 g) sugar

½ cup (175 g) honey

¼ cup (60ml) apple cider vinegar

1 tablespoon fennel seeds

2 lemons, zested and halved

1 teaspoon salt flakes

1 small fennel bulb, fronds reserved

1 large bunch Tuscan kale, about 250 g (9 oz)

1 tablespoon extra virgin olive oil

BP VINAIGRETTE

1 golden shallot (see page 17),
   finely diced

½ teaspoon dijon mustard

¼ cup (60 ml) extra virgin olive oil

FINAL BITS & BOBS

200 g (7 oz) creamy ricotta

¼ cup (40 g) sunflower seeds,
   well toasted

FRIENDS WITH

Pistou-roasted radishes with lentils p142

Use a slotted spoon to remove the pear and beetroot from the pot, reserving the poaching syrup. Cut the pear halves into wedgy quarters.

Make the BP vinaigrette by putting the juice of the remaining three lemon halves (about ¼ cup or 60 ml) and the shallot into a jar with ¼ cup (60 ml) of the reserved poaching syrup (save the rest for the shrub below), the mustard and oil, and give it all a good shake to combine. Pour over the relaxed kale and toss well to coat. Taste and season with salt and pepper. Add half of the pears and beetroot and toss again.

Tumble onto a serving platter and arrange the remaining pear and beetroot jauntily around the place, then blob on bits of ricotta and scatter with the reserved fennel fronds and toasted sunflower seeds.

BONUS RECIPE
SERVES 2–4

500 ml (2 cups) leftover poaching syrup

Ice cubes

Soda water, to taste

BP shrub

Strain out the fennel seeds from the poaching syrup.

Transfer to a clean jar with a tight-fitting lid and store in the fridge for up to 4 weeks.

To serve, splash some shrub over ice and top with soda water.

Here is a special occasion salad that deserves to be put on a pedestal. Leave it in the fridge until guests are sitting down, then bring it to the table for maximum showstopping effect. A 'shuba' is a fur coat: the 'fur' in question is a fuzzy grating of hardboiled egg. Herring is the kind of fishy fish that'll put hairs on your chest, especially if it's accompanied in the traditional way, with a shot of vodka (because fish like to swim). If you're new to it, or already an aficionado (a-fish-ionado?), shuba is the perfect festive wrapping. If you don't fancy herring, replace with shredded hot-smoked trout, or leave the fish out altogether: there are enough flavours going on here for everyone to be happy. Beetroot varies in size, so cooking time will, too, but they're ready when you can stick a fork all the way through. You can use vac-packed cooked beets instead, or even grated tinned baby beets would work – just drain on paper towel before adding. My Babushka Raya would always eat her shuba on very dark rye, so slip some slices in to serve. Think of it as a savoury salad cake centrepiece decorated with whatever you have to hand: sliced radish, cuke ribbons, dill fronds, caviar and (very optional, very va-va-voom) violets. Or make it in a trifle dish with grated egg on top. To your health: *Na zdarovya!*

Shuba salad

Pop beetroot (skin and all) into a saucepan of cold salted water and bring it to the boil, then drop to a simmer and cook for about an hour until fork-tender. Drain and leave to steam dry. When cool enough to handle, use paper towel or oiled fingers to swipe off the skin, then grate on the coarsest holes of a box grater and toss with the vinegar and sugar in a bowl. Set aside to cool completely.

Put the potatoes and carrots in another saucepan of cold salted water and bring to the boil, then drop to a simmer and cook until just tender, which'll take 20–25 minutes. Drain and steam dry in the pan, then peel off the skins of both veg using paper towel for added friction. When cool, grate the carrots and potatoes separately on the coarsest holes of a box grater and set aside in separate containers.

For the herby layer, combine the ingredients in a small bowl, stirring about to evenly distribute.

To make the creamy coat, combine all of the ingredients in a large bowl, and use a whisk to whip in enough air to stiffen the mixture and make it billowy and glossy. The flavour will develop over time, so don't be tempted to add extra salt. Pop into the fridge to help it set even more.

Find a platter or cake stand that'll comfortably fit a 20 cm (8 inch) springform cake tin, and have everything ready to go before you start to assemble.

RAINBOW VEG LAYER

400 g (14 oz) beetroot (beets), scrubbed

2 teaspoons apple cider vinegar

1 teaspoon caster (superfine) sugar

4–5 larger kipfler (fingerling) potatoes, about 500 g (1 lb 2 oz), scrubbed

3 carrots

300 g (10½ oz) herring fillets in oil, thinly sliced

½ small red onion, finely sliced into rings

4 eggs, hardboiled and peeled

HERBY LAYER

1 large dill pickle, coarsely grated

2 tablespoons dill, finely chopped

1 tablespoon finely snipped chives

1 tablespoon capers, finely chopped

1 tablespoon grated horseradish

Freshly ground black pepper

CREAMY COAT

400 g (14 oz) crème fraîche

¾ cup (185 g) whole egg mayonnaise

2 teaspoons dijon mustard

1 teaspoon lemon zest (1 small lemon's worth)

¼ teaspoon garlic powder

¼ teaspoon ground white pepper

½ teaspoon salt flakes

FINAL BITS & BOBS

Decorations, such as sliced radish, cucumber ribbons, dill fronds, caviar and edible flowers

To assemble the layers, place the grated beetroot into the bottom of the cake tin, smoothing off with the back of a spoon or offset spatula, giving it a gentle press to set. Spoon over ¼ cup of the creamy coat and smooth this off with the back of a spoon or offset spatula.

Arrange the slices of herring in an even layer over the creamy coat, then add the onion rings. Scatter the herby layer on top of the onion. Coarsely grate 3 of the eggs (reserving 1 for garnish) as the next layer straight into the tin, pressing down gently.

Pour another ¼ cup of creamy coat over the egg, and smooth. Arrange the carrot layer over this, then the potato and press down resolutely.

Get a plate and weigh it down for an hour or so in the fridge to chill and set before you put the final creamy coat on (you can leave this for a day in the fridge if need be).

When it comes time to wrap it in its creamy coat, place the serving platter or cake stand onto the top of the tin, then flip it over like you're turning out a cake. Unhinge the springform tin, and use an offset spatula or palette knife to smooth any roughage or rogue riff-raff. Press some paper towel into the beetroot to soak up any excess beet juices if you want to keep the coat snowy white (or leave it juicy if you'd prefer the coat to go pink).

Dollop most of the creamy coat on top and smooth it over as you would icing on a cake. Use an offset spatula to push the rest of the mix evenly across the top and down the sides. Use a clean cloth dampened with vinegar to clear any plate schmears.

As for the fur coat, finely grate the reserved hardboiled egg over, using the microplane you'd usually use for parmesan, then decorate to your heart's content.

Serve as a show-stopping centrepiece, slicing into wedges and using a cake server to dish it out.

FRIENDS WITH

Kind of a big dill p213

Every Sunday since before I can remember, we've had fish and potatoes for breakfast: herring in oil, smoked mackerel, sardines or some lazy lox, plus some tender tubers and slivers of shallot or red onion. You could use any tinned or smoked fish, or you could also just pull the fish out and keep it vego. If you don't have caperberries, use capers, and feel free to fry some to sprinkle on top as well. If this salad is travelling, swap the cos for rocket (washed and chilled). We've prepared it here as a help-yourself reconstruction, but if you'd prefer to toss everything together in a bowl before plonking onto a platter, that is always a winner.

Scandi breakfast salad

Put the potato in a steamer basket and steam for 20 minutes or until fork-tender.

Make the crème fraîche tartare by whisking all of the ingredients together, then taste and season with more salt and pepper as required.

Separate the cos into leaves, slicing larger leaves if you so desire (I do like the drama of a long leaf, mind you).

When the potato is cool enough to handle, toss gently in a few tablespoons of the tartare, then arrange in a bowl with the lemon segments, cos leaves and olive oil, and season with salt and pepper.

Break up the trout and serve on top of the salad or on the side. Serve the remainder of the tartare in a bowl so that people can help themselves, along with the radishes, caperberries, reserved onion slices and reserved herbs.

750 g (1 lb 10 oz) kipfler (fingerling) potatoes, sliced on the bias 1 cm (⅜ inch) thick

1 tall cos (romaine) lettuce, soaked in chilled water

1 lemon, peeled and cut into segments

2 tablespoons extra virgin olive oil, plus extra for finishing

250 g (9 oz) hot-smoked ocean trout fillet

CRÈME FRAÎCHE TARTARE

200 g (7 oz) crème fraîche

½ small red onion, finely diced, finely slicing the other half for garnish

Zest and juice of 1 lemon

2–3 cornichons, finely diced

1½ tablespoons horseradish cream

1 tablespoon finely diced caperberries

1 handful chopped parsley leaves, plus extra whole leaves for serving

½ handful chopped dill, plus extra fronds for serving

1 teaspoon salt flakes

¼ teaspoon freshly cracked black pepper

FINAL BITS & BOBS

1 bunch breakfast radishes, about 250 g (7 oz), halved lengthways

¼ cup (50 g) caperberries, stems attached, halved lengthways

FRIENDS WITH

Silverbeet & broccoli tumble with herby avocado dressing p220

This is a cracker of a potato salad, thanks to the crispy crunchy cracked skins, and its zero-waste credentials. Chat potatoes are best, because they're an early pick; still firm enough to hold their shape, but will soften through the middles for a totally textural experience. The dressing is a delicious way to use up your herbs, even if they're a bit wilty. Whatever you have in the soft herb department is welcome. If you've only got big green olives instead of kalamata, they'll do the trick as well. Make this planty by using a crumbly vegan cheese (or a marinated one) instead.

Potato crack salad
with feta crumble

1 kg (2 lb 4 oz) chat potatoes

1 teaspoon salt flakes

Parsley and soft herb stems, reserved from the dressing (see below)

2 garlic cloves

¼ cup (60 ml) extra virgin olive oil

125 g (4½ oz) kalamata olives, pitted

SOFT HERB DRESSING

1 cup tightly packed parsley leaves

½ cup tightly packed soft herbs such as dill, mint, chives, basil or small tarragon leaves

1 cup (250 ml) just-boiled water from the potatoes

1 garlic clove

½ cup (125 ml) extra virgin olive oil

1 heaped tablespoon seeded mustard

1 tablespoon red wine vinegar

1 cup tightly packed baby spinach leaves (optional but excellent)

FINAL BITS & BOBS

100 g (3½ oz) crumbly feta

1 red onion, finely sliced

Put chat potatoes in a saucepan along with salt, the herb stems and garlic cloves, cover with cold water, bring to the boil, then simmer for 15–20 minutes or until fork-tender.

Fish out the potatoes, reserving the just-boiled water along with the garlic cloves and herb stems.

Preheat the oven to 220°C (430°F) or 200°C (400°F) fan forced, with the baking tray inside.

Toss the potatoes with oil and a good pinch of salt flakes, not minding if the skins get a little chuffed up (this'll only make them crispier!). Tip onto the hot tray along with the olives and use the base of a jar to give each potato a firm squish to flatten them a little, creating cracks, without pressing so hard that they break up.

Roast for 25–30 minutes for the potatoes to frizzle on their cracked skins and the olives to blister.

To make the soft herb dressing, put the herb leaves in a heatproof colander and pour the reserved potato water over the top, reuniting the herb stems and cooked garlic with the rest of the herbs.

Transfer the contents of the drained colander, along with the fresh garlic into a small blender with the olive oil, mustard, vinegar and baby spinach (if using). Blitz until super smooth. Taste and season with salt and pepper.

Toss through the hot crack potatoes and pitted olives, letting them sit for a beat to absorb the dressing. Transfer to a salad bowl or platter and crumble with feta and a tumble of the finely sliced onion before serving warm.

FRIENDS WITH

Piquant pantry salad with a few green bits p202

A classic comeback: devilled eggs are SO HOT RIGHT NOW, so why not saladify them? Egg salads are a staple of a Shabbos meal, and this has the added benefit of crunchy crudités and luscious leaves. The devil is in the detail. Using Japanese mayo oomphs up the umami, along with dijon or hot English mustard (if you dare!) for piquancy. Sriracha is a serving suggestion: use whatever hot sauce you have, and just leave a bottle by the bowl to sploosh over the top if some like it hot. You could easily use the leftovers as a sandwich filling, too, if you were that way inclined.

Devilled egg *and* baby spinach salad

To make the devilled egg dressing, bring a medium saucepan of water to a rolling boil, then gently place the eggs in the water using a slotted spoon, and drop the heat to a simmer to keep the eggs from partying too hard in the pan. Set the timer to 8 minutes for just on hardboiled. Scoop into cold water to stop the cooking and help with peeling (smashing from the blunt end first to help keep the egg intact).

While the eggs are cooking, combine the mayonnaise, mustard, garlic, hot sauce and lemon juice in a large bowl. Whisk together, then fold in the grated dill pickle and celery, along with half of the chives and dill sprigs (the rest is garnish). Taste and season with salt and pepper.

Peel the eggs, then dip them back into the eggy swimming pool to remove any shell grit. Dry then slice the eggs into rough cubes using a knife or an egg cutter, and set aside.

Drain and spin the baby spinach and reserved celery leaves dry, then arrange the leaves around the edges of the platter with wedges of drained and dried radish. Pile up the egg salad in the centre and garnish with the reserved chives and dill. Drizzle with olive oil, crack some extra pepper over, and serve with more hot sauce on the side.

50 g (1¾ oz) baby spinach leaves, soaked

4 radishes, cut into wedges and soaked in chilled water

DEVILLED EGG DRESSING

8 eggs, at room temperature

⅔ cup (165 g) Kewpie mayonnaise

1 tablespoon dijon mustard

1–2 garlic cloves, finely grated

¼ teaspoon Sriracha (or other hot sauce), or to taste

1 tablespoon lemon juice

1 large dill pickle, grated

1 celery heart, finely chopped, reserving the leaves in chilled water for garnish

2 tablespoons finely chopped chives, reserving half for garnish

5 dill sprigs, finely chopped, keeping half for garnish

½ teaspoon each of salt flakes and pepper

FINAL BITS & BOBS

Drizzle of extra virgin olive oil

Extra hot sauce (if you dare!)

FRIENDS WITH

Orange veg on green'd quinoa p170

Most of these ingredients come from the pantry, with a freshen up from some lemon and herbs. If you don't have any lemons, double the white wine vinegar and be generous with the honey, but if you've got a Meyer lemon, use THAT in the dressing for extra sweetness and aroma. This is even more delicious as leftovers the next day, and will last for days in the fridge. The green peas will have lost some of their brightness, but it's a small price to pay for a filling flavour bomb salad. To bulk it out further, add a medium tin of tuna, or an extra tin of beans or chickpeas. Preserved lemon is not a deal-breaker – leave it out if it saves you a trip to the shops.

Piquant pantry salad *with* a few green bits

To make the dressing, combine the garlic, vinegar, mustard, honey, preserved lemon and the salt and pepper in a large bowl and give it a good whisk to dissolve the salt and to get the emulsification going. Add the olive oil and the lemon zest and juice to taste. I like it very lemony.

Drop the four bean mix into the dressing, along with the capsicum, capers, olives and most of the sliced onion, reserving some for the top.

Put 2 cups (500 ml) of well-salted water in a small saucepan and bring to the boil. Add the peas, return to the boil, and simmer for 2–3 minutes until tender. Drain well and toss through the salad while hot, along with the parsley and dill, to get friendly.

Pour onto a shallow serving bowl and dress with reserved onion rings and dill fronds. Serve warm or at room temperature with lemon cheeks alongside.

400 g (14 oz) tin four bean mix, drained and rinsed

350 g (12 oz) grilled marinated capsicum (peppers), sliced

1 tablespoon capers, rinsed and drained

12 stuffed green olives, sliced in half

1 red onion, finely sliced into rings

200 g (7 oz) fresh or frozen peas (whatever you've got!)

½ cup chopped parsley leaves

¼ cup chopped dill, pretty fronds reserved for garnish

YOU'VE PROBABLY GOT THIS IN THE PANTRY DRESSING

2 garlic cloves, finely diced

1 tablespoon white wine vinegar

1 tablespoon dijon mustard

1 teaspoon honey

1 tablespoon preserved lemon cheek, rind only, finely diced

¼ teaspoon salt flakes

¼ teaspoon freshly cracked black pepper

¼ cup (60 ml) extra virgin olive oil

Zest and juice of 1 lemon

FINAL BITS & BOBS

Lemon cheeks

FRIENDS WITH

Potato crack salad with feta crumble p199

These are unapologetically a side, because sometimes you need SOMETHING else to go with your more substantial salads. Once you've got the timings on this one in the bag, you'll be able to blanch and toss to your heart's content. The best part about green beans is that you can cook 'em from fresh or frozen with equal success: spring and summer into early autumn for fresh beans, and the rest of the time I'll see you in the freezer aisle. I slightly undercook my beans to let the residual heat do the work; they're still hot enough to soak up the dressing, and I don't have to muck about with bowls of iced water. If you're worried you've overcooked yours, run them under cold water to cool them down. Also, worry less. They're just beans. You can use a bean splitter to halve the cooking time – and topping and snapping is a fun job to entrust the kiddies with!

Blanch 'n' toss beans

Put 2 litres (8 cups) water and the salt in a large saucepan with some height still available for bubbling, then bring it to the boil.

Top the beans (that's nipping off the stalky end with a twist of your fingers or a knife), no need to tail. If they're lengthy beans, snap them in half (I like to outsource this to tiny hands); if beans are smaller, leave them whole. Give them a quick rinse and plonk into the water, using the lid of the pot as a shield if you're worried about splashing.

Drain after 4 minutes for al dente, after 5 minutes for a slightly less toothsome bean.

Pop in a bowl and toss with one of the following dressings:

Lemony toss

Shake all the ingredients in a jar and toss through warm beans.

Chilli butter toss

Melt butter in a medium saucepan over a medium-low heat and, when it starts to foam, add the chilli and garlic. Wait for the aroma to hit your nostrils, then switch off the heat and toss the warm beans through the chilli butter.

Honey miso toss

Pop all ingredients except the toasted sesame seeds in a bowl and whisk to a creamy caramel brown. Toss through the still-warm beans and sprinkle with sesame seeds.

1 tablespoon salt flakes

500 g (1 lb 2 oz) green beans

LEMONY TOSS

Zest and juice of 1 lemon

2–3 garlic cloves, minced

¼ cup (60 ml) extra virgin olive oil

¼ teaspoon salt flakes

1 pinch caster (superfine) sugar

CHILLI BUTTER TOSS

75 g (2¾ oz) salted butter

1 long red chilli, finely chopped (or 1 tablespoon chilli flakes)

2–3 garlic cloves, minced

HONEY MISO TOSS

1 tablespoon miso paste

1–2 garlic cloves, minced (or ½ teaspoon garlic powder)

1½ teaspoons (about a knuckle) minced ginger

1 teaspoon honey

1 tablespoon sesame oil

½ teaspoon salt flakes

1 tablespoon sesame seeds, toasted

FRIENDS WITH

Cauli korma crown and cardamom brown rice p178

HONEY MISO TOSS

LEMONY TOSS

CHILLI BUTTER TOSS

YAMPERS (CAMPER'S
JACKET YAMS)
(PAGE 160)

KIPFLERS AND GREEN
BEANS DRESSED BY
ALMONDINE (PAGE 214)

**HONEYED BUTTERNUT RISONI
SALAD WITH MARINATED FETA
(PAGE 163)**

**KIND OF A BIG DILL
(PAGE 213)**

This spice mix, known as Svanskaya Sol, is so precious to Georgians that it's even been given UNESCO heritage listing. It originates from a mountainous, rugged part of Georgia, where it's useful for zhuzhing up even the plainest veg. I've used flat beans here, because they're inexpensive and forgiving if you can find them, but you can keep it simple with some green or yellow beans (even from the freezer). If you don't have hot paprika, use cayenne or just leave it out. We're using the blender rather than a spice blender for the Svanetia salt because it doesn't have to be fine – even a mortar and pestle will do it (and is probably the most authentic method if you've got the time).

Braised flat beans *with* Svanetia-spiced walnuts

To make the Svanetia salt, put the coriander and caraway seeds into a large frying pan and heat over medium heat for 2–3 minutes until the spices give off a toasty, nutty aroma. Transfer to a small blender along with the fenugreek and cayenne, and pulse a few times until the seeds smash up a little and turn to a light tan coarse powder.

Toss the half cup of walnuts into the still-warm pan and shimmy about on a low to medium heat for 2–3 minutes until the tips start to turn golden. Chuck the spices and salt into the pan with the olive oil to help coat the nuts. Transfer to a plate to cool.

Top beans and string, if needed, then put them into a steamer. Steam with a lid on for 10 minutes, or until just tender. Drain (reserving some of the cooking water). Leave uncovered to steam dry.

To make the creamy walnut dressing, using the same large pan you used for the spices, add the olive oil and sweat the onion, garlic, walnuts, salt and pepper for 15 minutes with the lid on until onion is soft and starting to colour, shimmying it about every now and again.

Coarsely chop the basil and coriander stems, along with some of the larger basil leaves, saving prettier little ones and the coriander leaves for garnish. Add the stems and spices to the onion mixture and continue to sauté for another minute.

Transfer the onion mixture to a small blender and whiz up with the red wine vinegar and ¼ cup (60 ml) of the reserved bean water. Taste, season with salt and pepper, and toss with the well-drained and steam-dried beans to coat. Transfer to a serving bowl, drizzle with some extra olive oil and scatter with the Svanetia-spiced walnuts and the reserved basil and coriander leaves. Serve warm or cold.

1 kg (2 lb 4 oz) flat beans

SVANETIA SALT-SPICED WALNUTS

2 teaspoons coriander seeds

1 teaspoon caraway seeds

½ teaspoon ground fenugreek

1 pinch cayenne pepper

½ cup (50 g) fresh walnuts

1 teaspoon salt flakes

1 tablespoon extra virgin olive oil

CREAMY WALNUT DRESSING

2 tablespoons extra virgin olive oil, plus extra for drizzling

1 brown onion, diced

2 garlic cloves, bruised and peeled

1 cup (100 g) fresh walnuts

½ teaspoon each salt flakes and freshly ground pepper

3 Thai basil stems, leaves picked and reserved

3 coriander (cilantro) stems, leaves picked and reserved

½ teaspoon ground cumin

1 teaspoon ground coriander

¼ teaspoon ground cinnamon

1 tablespoon red wine vinegar

FRIENDS WITH

Roasted beets with spiced walnuts & Georgian garo p187

You'll love this SPC (sesame-peanut-chilli) dressing so much, you'll wish you could buy it in a jar. This salad works best if you can find long, languid veg, such as kai lan (Chinese broccoli), snake beans and even spring onions! The theatre comes in bringing the lot to the table, along with a pair of scissors or kitchen shears to let guests snip at the salad themselves. Serve this one hot or cold, over rice or noodles, or as a simple side with other dishes, and extra SPC dressing on the side.

SPC long green veg

Bring a large saucepan of well-salted water to the boil.

Meanwhile, to make the SPC dressing, pop the sesame seeds and peanuts into a cold wok or large heavy-based frying pan, then turn the heat to medium-low and continue to toss and stir until they are golden brown. This will only take about 3 minutes, so keep the seeds and peanuts moving the whole time (don't walk away). When done, transfer to a medium heatproof bowl, making sure every last seed is scooped, and set aside.

Turn the heat up to medium-high and pour in all of the peanut oil, then wait for it to heat up until shimmering. Add the shallots, stir-frying for 2–3 minutes, then add the garlic, ginger and red chilli and stir-fry for a minute, tossing about in the pan until the shallots are transparent and starting to caramelise. Add the chilli flakes and give everything a good stir. Transfer to the heatproof bowl with the sesame seeds and peanuts, and leave to get friendly.

Once the water has boiled, blanch the kai lan and snake beans for 2 minutes until vibrantly green. Drain through a heatproof colander and run under a cold tap to stop the cooking process. Transfer to paper towel to pat dry.

Wipe out the wok or pan and crank the heat to high, pour in the peanut oil and drop in the blanched, dried green stuff to stir-fry for 2 minutes (in batches if your pan is on the smaller side), then transfer to a mixing bowl. Splash with sesame oil and toss about to coat. Transfer to a serving platter.

Scoop the SPC dressing back into the wok. Listen for a sizzle, then pour in the soy sauce, shaoxing rice wine, sugar and vinegar, which should boil instantly. Continue to burble together for 1 minute before pouring over the greens.

If you're up for some tableside theatre, provide your guests with kitchen shears to chop the lengths of beans and brocc into thirds. Or, for ease of use, chop the lengths into thirds before topping with sauce. Serve warm or cooled.

2 bunches kai lan (Chinese broccoli), about 600 g (1 lb 5 oz), bases trimmed, thicker stalks and bigger leaves sliced vertically in half

300 g (10½ oz) snake beans

2 tablespoons peanut oil

1 tablespoon sesame oil

SPC (SESAME-PEANUT-CHILLI) DRESSING

½ cup (70 g) sesame seeds

⅔ cup (150 g) roasted peanuts

½ cup (125 ml) peanut oil

4 banana shallots (see page 17), finely sliced with the grain

4 garlic cloves, finely sliced

1 thumb ginger, julienned

1 long red chilli, finely sliced

1 tablespoon chilli flakes

2 tablespoons light soy sauce

1 tablespoon shaoxing rice wine

1 tablespoon sugar

1 teaspoon rice wine vinegar

FRIENDS WITH

Sticky eggplant, tofu and noodle salad p182

There is, frankly, nothing better than a Pickle Party (see page 13 for a selection of my favourites). I've employed Adelaide chef Simon Bryant's tip of chilling the cucumbers to make them easier to grill without turning mushy. Taste the rose harissa on the day to make amends: it can be fiery. You can use dried rose harissa or paste – whatever you've already bought for Ottolenghifying. This uses half a pack of baby cucumbers, so use the rest for lunchboxes or a crudité platter. Smetana means sour cream in Russian. Buckwheat can vary, so it's best to get yours from a continental deli in your Bagel Belt, or swap for a 400 g (14 oz) tin of chickpeas, tossed through the harissa and toasted.

Kind of a big dill

4 Lebanese cucumbers, about 600 g (1 lb 5 oz), peeled and cut in half

4 dill pickles, brine reserved for dressing, cut in half

½ cup (100 g) toasted buckwheat kasha groats

1 tablespoon extra virgin olive oil, plus extra for finishing

1–2 tablespoons rose harissa

HERBY SMETANA DRESSING

½ cup (130 g) sour cream

2 tablespoons pickle brine (see above)

1 tablespoon extra virgin olive oil

1–2 garlic cloves, minced

1 teaspoon runny honey

¼ cup (20 g) chopped dill, reserving pretty fronds for garnish

1 mint sprig, chopped, reserving smaller leaves for garnish

4 parsley sprigs, chopped, reserving some leaves for garnish

Zest and juice of 1 lemon

½ teaspoon salt flakes

¼ teaspoon freshly cracked black pepper

FINAL BITS & BOBS

250 g (9 oz) baby cucumbers, cut diagonally on the bias

Put Lebanese cucumbers and dill pickles on a tray and into the freezer while you potter about (for a maximum time of 1 hour, or they'll be a little too chilled).

To cook the buckwheat, bring 1½ cups (325 ml) of well-salted water to the boil in a small saucepan. Add the buckwheat and olive oil to the boiling water, wait for it to come back to the boil, then drop to a low simmer and cover with the lid for 14 minutes or until all of the liquid has absorbed and the buckwheat groats are softened. Spoon in the rose harissa, and fluff about with a fork to coat.

Preheat the oven to 200°C (400°F) or 180°C (350°F) fan forced and line a baking tray with baking paper.

Tumble the harissa'd buckwheat onto the baking tray and sprinkle with salt flakes. Toast in the oven for 10 minutes or until crispy, giving it the odd stir about to break up.

Heat a griddle pan or barbecue grill until smoking. Brush the chilled cucumbers and dill pickles with olive oil and place them cut-side down on the hot griddle for 4–5 minutes to get some char marks. Use something heavy to weigh them down if you're impatient.

Make the herby smetana dressing by combining the sour cream with the pickle brine in a mixing bowl. Add the olive oil, garlic, honey, herbs, lemon zest and juice, salt and pepper. Whisk well, taste and season with more salt and pepper if needed.

Pour dressing into a serving jug or bowl. Tumble the spiced buckwheat into the base of a wide shallow bowl. Arrange the warm cucumbers and dill pickles over the top, along with the baby cucumbers, sprinkling with the reserved herbs and a drizzle of extra olive oil for good measure. Take to the table and toss the dressing through the salad to watch the magic happen (more magic to come when you taste it).

FRIENDS WITH

Shuba salad p192

Invest in this kinda bitcoin, where the bits are potato, and your dividends are dinner: low risk, high return. Shocking the beans, then baking the lot is a foolproof way of ensuring everything is tender and perfectly cooked. This one's a hot dressing, and it's best served warm. Foaming the butter with capers and almonds is seriously sumptuous, and you'll want to make this to pour over delicate proteins such as fish, shellfish or chicken, which you're welcome to cook alongside this salad as well. Parsley is an easy go-to soft herb here, but you could use chervil or tarragon or dill – I've just put too much dill in this book already.

Kipflers *and* green beans dressed by Almondine

Preheat the oven to 220°C (430°F) or 200°C (400°F) fan forced with a baking tray inside.

In a bowl, toss the kipfler coins in 1 tablespoon of the olive oil with some salt flakes and freshly ground pepper.

Once the oven's hot, remove the tray with gloves, and carefully drape with baking paper. Scatter the coins over the tray, pop into the oven and roast for about 15 minutes until the potato starts to colour and can be pricked with a fork.

While the potatoes are roasting, bring 2 cups (500 ml) of water to the boil. Put the beans in a heatproof bowl and pour the boiling water over them, then leave for a minute. Strain through a heatproof colander and leave them to steam dry and continue cooking through. Toss prepared beans in the remaining tablespoon of olive oil, with some salt flakes and freshly ground pepper.

When the potato discs have coloured, shuffle them to the side and add the prepared beans to the tray.

Turn down heat to 200°C (400°F) or 180°C (350°F) fan forced and return the tray to the oven to cook for 5–7 minutes. The beans should be crisp-tender.

Place the potato first on a warmed platter, then the beans, and pour any pan juices over. Toss the lemon zest over the salad.

To make the almondine dressing, foam the butter in a small frying pan, then toss in the capers and wait until they crisp up and start to unfurl. Scoop out and reserve. Add a splash of extra olive oil along with the garlic, shallot and almonds to the pan. Cook over gentle heat until the garlic starts to brown, then remove from the heat and add the lemon juice, swirling to incorporate. Taste and season with salt and pepper.

Pour the dressing over the salad, scatter with the parsley and reserved crispy capers and serve warm with lemon wedges on the side.

500 g (1 lb 4 oz) kipfler (fingerling) potatoes, cut into 1 cm (⅜ inch) coins

2 tablespoons extra virgin olive oil, plus extra for the dressing

400 g (14 oz) green beans, topped

Zest of 1 lemon

ALMONDINE DRESSING

50 g (1¾ oz) butter

2 tablespoons lilliput capers, rinsed and drained

2 garlic cloves, thinly sliced

1 golden shallot (see page 17), thinly sliced

½ cup (50 g) flaked almonds

Juice of 1 lemon

FINAL BITS & BOBS

Handful parsley leaves, finely shredded

Lemon wedges

FRIENDS WITH

Hot cheeseboard salad with honey—walnut dressing p130

What's the difference between this and a stir-fry? It's served in a salad bowl, at room temp! A bit like eating last night's stir-fry for breakfast (also welcome and encouraged). It's the kind of stir-fry salad you're going to want to make all year round, so if Asian greens aren't forthcoming, or you've got baby broccoli (broccolini), asparagus or snow peas handy, these would be fantastic here too. Bok choy is notoriously sandy between its sheets, so tear the leaves off the base and rinse and soak judiciously. The cabbage stays raw here to make an extra fresh juxtaposition against the par-cooked veg. If you don't have cashew nuts, use macadamia or for a nut-free alternative, try sliced water chestnuts.

Broccoli *and* cashew salad-fry

Finely shred cabbage and put it into a large bowl.

Boil 2 cups (500 ml) of water. Cut the broccoli into small florets, then peel and finely slice the stem. Cut the bok choy into 2 cm (¾ inch) lengths. Par-cook the broccoli and bok choy by putting them in a heatproof colander or sieve with a bowl beneath it, then pouring the boiling water over. Leave the veg in the colander to steam dry. Reserve the water in the bowl.

Plunge the noodles into the bowl of reserved water for a minute, shimmying them about with tongs to separate, then drain well.

To make the cashew soy dressing, blitz all of the ingredients in a small blender until combined into a smooth slurry.

Heat the neutral oil in a wok or heavy-based well-seasoned frying pan. Add the spring onion batons for a minute to flavour the oil, then add the broccoli and the bok choy and stir-fry for a minute, working in batches if your wok or pan isn't big enough to allow for some space between bits. Tip into the bowl with the cabbage.

Pour the dressing into the hot wok and bring to the boil. The sauce should be silky and glossy, which will happen almost instantly.

Add the drained noodles to the wok with the sauce, along with the cashews and sesame seeds and toss around to coat in the dressing. Splash in another ¼ cup (60 ml) of water and allow this to incorporate, then transfer to the mixing bowl with the vegetables and add the coriander leaves.

Toss everything together, season with salt and pepper, and transfer to a shallow platter. Serve at room temperature, sprinkled with extra sesame seeds, flanked by lemon wedges.

¼ head curly cabbage such as wombok or savoy, about 400 g (14 oz)

1 broccoli head, about 300 g (10½ oz)

1 bunch (2–3 heads) bok choy

200 g (7 oz) fresh chow mein noodles

2 tablespoons neutral oil (I like grapeseed or peanut)

4 spring onions (scallions), sliced into 5 cm (2 inch) batons

¼ cup (40 g) toasted cashews

2 tablespoons well-toasted sesame seeds, plus extra for garnish if desired

1 cup loosely packed coriander (cilantro) leaves, stems reserved for the dressing

CASHEW SOY DRESSING

1 thumb of ginger, finely grated

3 garlic cloves

Reserved coriander stems (see above)

¼ cup (40 g) toasted cashews

3 tablespoons sesame oil

2 tablespoons oyster sauce

2 tablespoons lemon juice

1 tablespoon light soy sauce

1 tablespoon shaoxing rice wine

1 tablespoon sweet chilli sauce

½ teaspoon salt flakes

½ cup (125 ml) just-boiled water (and more on standby)

FINAL BITS & BOBS

1 lemon, cut into wedges

FRIENDS WITH

Miso-roasted cauli with broad bean smash p164

The self-saucing element here is the bain-marie bowl of dressing and chickpeas gently warming over the top of the blanching water. Once you start to whiff a waft of the wonderful garlicky-lemony aroma emanating from the bowl, you'll want to take a little bathe in it yourself. I've kept the dressing anchovy-free to accommodate plant-based friends – just skip the parm when finishing. But if you're looking for permission to add six or so anchovy fillets, along with a good wodge of butter, this is it. If you'd like to triple-down on green veg, feel free to include a medley, such as green beans, asparagus, broccoli and even raw zucchini.

Broccolini *with* self-saucing chickpeas

3 bunches broccolini, sliced on the bias into 3 cm (1¼ inch) batons

SELF-SAUCING CHICKPEAS

1 lemon

400 g (14 oz) tin chickpeas, drained and rinsed

4 marinated artichoke hearts, quartered

3 garlic cloves, finely sliced

½ cup (85 g) stuffed green olives, halved

1 teaspoon mild chilli flakes

½ cup (125 ml) extra virgin olive oil

1 tablespoon red wine vinegar

1 tablespoon dijon mustard

½ teaspoon salt flakes and freshly ground pepper

FINAL BITS & BOBS

40 g (1½ oz) parmesan cheese, shaved

½ cup (50 g) flaked almonds, toasted

To make the self-saucing chickpeas, find a medium saucepan and a metal bowl that comfortably fits over it. Peel the lemon as close to the zest as possible and scrape any pith off the skin with a teaspoon. Cut the lemon into cheeks and reserve for a garnish. Finely slice the peel and put it into the metal bowl with the remaining self-sauced chickpeas ingredients, stirring about to introduce everyone to each other.

Half-fill the saucepan beneath with well-salted water and heat on medium-low (make sure there's enough height clearance so the water won't start bubbling over once the bowl's on top). Place the bowl of chickpea mixture over the top and allow to gently heat together while the water comes to the boil.

When the water comes to the boil, remove and set aside the chickpea bowl (taking care as it may be hot), chuck the broccolini into the pan and set the timer for 3–4 minutes (depending on the thickness of your broccolini stems).

Once the broccolini has cooked, tong it into the chickpea mixture in the bowl, tossing about to get friendly, then transfer to a shallow platter for serving. Taste and season with salt and pepper. Finish with shavings of fresh parmesan, toasted almonds and the reserved lemon cheeks on the side for acid trippers.

Serve hot or at room temperature – it's all good, so do what you wanna do.

FRIENDS WITH

Charred capsicum on feta & butterbean purée p177

Green on green on green is good. Grapes' tart sweetness with the bitter earthiness of the silverbeet is all brought together with a creamy, zippy avocado tahini (which is totally a tahini guac). It's very #health without feeling like you're going without. You're only using the silverbeet leaves here, so chop the stalks to sweat with onion for any kind of stew or soup, anywhere you'd use celery (you can also freeze for 'ron). If you can't be bothered slicing with precision, cut the brocc into chunks and pulse in a food processor. Add as much garlic as you want – I like mine garlicky, obvs.

Silverbeet & broccoli tumble *with* herby avocado dressing

Boil 2 cups (500 ml) of water. Trim and peel the broccoli stem, then slice it thinly along with the florets, following the shape of the broccoli. Do the same with the fennel bulb. Pop both into a heatproof colander and pour the boiling water over the top.

Roll the silverbeet leaves up and thinly shred with your sharp knife. Rub the leaves with the olive oil and a pinch of salt flakes to macerate.

To make the dressing, blitz all of the herby avocado dressing ingredients in a food processor to a thin paste. Taste and season with more salt and pepper if needed.

Toss the drained veg, rubbed silverbeet and the grapes together in a serving dish, then drizzle generously with the dressing (feel free to leave any leftovers in a jug on the table) and finish with a sprinkle of pepitas, reserved spring onion whites and fennel fronds.

1 broccoli head

1 small fennel bulb, about 200 g (7 oz), fronds reserved for garnish

½ bunch silverbeet (Swiss chard), leaves only

2 tablespoons extra virgin olive oil

300 g (10½ oz) green grapes, halved

HERBY AVOCADO DRESSING

2 spring onions (scallions), green parts only, white parts finely sliced and reserved

½ cup coarsely chopped dill

½ cup coarsely chopped parsley leaves

¼ cup (60 ml) extra virgin olive oil

1–2 garlic cloves

2 tablespoons apple cider vinegar

1 ripe avocado (a creamier variety like Hass)

1 tablespoon tahini

1 teaspoon dijon mustard

Zest and juice of 1 lemon

1 teaspoon salt flakes

½ teaspoon freshly cracked black pepper

FINAL BITS & BOBS

2 tablespoons pepitas (pumpkin seeds), toasted

FRIENDS WITH
Scandi breakfast salad p196

The advantage of a recipe that frames an entire family of veg as options is that you've no excuse but to make this one. You could use broccolini, broccoli, double the Brussels sprouts, or go heavy on the kohlrabi – or whatever other brassica catches your eye at the shops is welcome here. Agrodolce means sour–sweet, and the dressing – a combination of balsamic and seeded mustard for acidity with sweetness from honey and currants – is gorgeously balanced against the burnished bitterness of the cruciferous veg and the velvetiness of the macadamia cream. You could serve this one hot or cold, and make the macadamia cream a day in advance; just give it a good whip before schmearing.

Agrodolce roasted brassicas *with* macadamia cream

Preheat oven to 220°C (430°F) or 200°C (400°F) fan forced. Prepare 2 baking trays. While the oven is heating, spread the macadamias for the final bits and bobs onto one of the trays and then pop both of the trays into the oven to preheat. Set the timer for 10 minutes, then pull the macas out, coarsely chop and reserve. Pop the tray back in and let the oven come to temperature (this may vary slightly depending on how quickly your oven heats up, so just keep an eye out).

Make the macadamia cream by draining the macas and putting the softened nuts into a blender along with the vinegar, oil, salt flakes and ½ cup (125 ml) of water (preferably filtered). Blitz until super smooth, adding extra salt and some pepper to taste. Scrape out into a bowl and set aside to chill in the fridge.

In a mixing bowl, toss the Brussels sprouts and the kohlrabi with olive oil, salt and pepper. Place the Brussels sprouts cut-side down on one of the preheated trays (hot!) and place the kohlrabi chunks on the other tray. Roast with the kohlrabi in the middle and Brussels sprouts on the top shelf of the oven for 15–20 minutes undisturbed, until the sprouts are golden brown and crispy on the outside and tender in the middle. Once you pull the sprouts out, bring the kohlrabi up to the top of the oven and give it another 5–10 minutes to crisp up.

Toss the reserved outer sprout leaves with another tablespoon of oil in the tossing bowl, then pop them into the oven for 10 minutes to become crispy and burnished.

Meanwhile, using the tossing bowl again, mix together the agrodolce dressing ingredients, reserving half of the chives for serving.

When the vegetables are done, toss immediately through the agrodolce dressing.

Swadge the chilled macadamia cream onto a shallow platter and tumble the glazed brassicas over. Dress with reserved chives, chopped macadamias and some salt flakes and freshly ground pepper.

600 g (1 lb 5oz) Brussels sprouts, trimmed and halved, outer leaves reserved

2 kohlrabi, about 800 g (1 lb 12 oz), peeled and sliced into 1 cm x 3 cm (⅜ inch x 1¼ inch) chunks

¼ cup (60 ml) extra virgin olive oil, plus 1 tablespoon extra for the outer sprout leaves

MACADAMIA CREAM

1 cup (130 g) macadamias, soaked in 1 cup (250 ml) boiling water for 30 minutes

2 tablespoons white wine vinegar

¼ cup (60 ml) neutral oil (I like grapeseed or sunflower here)

1 teaspoon salt flakes

AGRODOLCE DRESSING

2 tablespoons balsamic vinegar

1 tablespoon seeded mustard

1 tablespoon runny honey

1 tablespoon capers, rinsed, drained and roughly chopped

¼ cup (40 g) currants

½ bunch chives, finely chopped

FINAL BITS & BOBS

¼ cup (30 g) macadamias

FRIENDS WITH

Eggplant and capsicum with fermented black bean dressing p134

Brown butter's fancy French name, beurre noisette, refers to hazelnut-brown, which makes hazelnuts a fitting and fabulous addition here. If you're a confident coordinator, feel free to try boiling the brocc at the same time as steaming the sprouts: they take the same amount of time. You could add a grain or pulse to bulk it out – peas, asparagus and broad beans would all be welcome additions. The anchovies act as seasoning and funk, so use the best you can afford. Because there's butter in the dressing, this one's best served warm. Olive oil could be an alternative if you want to serve it cool and dairy-free.

Brown-buttered brocc & Brussels *with* pecorino cloud

500 g (1 lb 2 oz) Brussels sprouts

1 broccoli head

200 g (7 oz) green beans

ANCHOVY & BROWN BUTTER TOSS

7 anchovy fillets

1 garlic clove, minced

½ teaspoon salt flakes

75 g (2¾ oz) unsalted butter

¼ cup (40 g) hazelnuts, toasted

¼ cup (60 ml) extra virgin olive oil, plus extra for finishing

¼ bunch each of dill and chives, leaves picked and chopped together finely, reserving half for garnish

FINAL BITS & BOBS

40 g (1½ oz) pecorino cheese

Cut the ends off the sprouts and shred against the grain to approximately 5 mm (¼ inch) thin strips. Break up the broccoli into florets, then cut these into small fork-sized bits. Peel and thinly slice the stem (or eat it raw as a chef's snack!). Top the beans, then slice them in half on the bias.

Make the anchovy and brown butter toss. Using your knife on a 45 degree angle, mash the anchovies, garlic and salt flakes together across a board to form a paste. Melt the butter in a small frying pan on medium heat, allowing it to foam and start to turn golden brown. When it smells like cookies, throw in the anchovy-garlic paste, the hazelnuts and the olive oil, stirring to combine. Turn off the heat, then fold through the herbs. Transfer to a medium heatproof bowl.

Bring a saucepan of well-salted water to the boil with a steamer insert handy. When water is at the boil, add the broccoli and beans and set the timer for 5 minutes. Set the steamer on top, add the Brussels sprouts and cover with a well-fitting lid. When the timer goes off, drain the veg well and transfer to the bowl with the anchovy and brown butter toss to get acquainted.

Transfer to a serving dish. Drizzle with a little extra olive oil, finely grate pecorino over the top as a cloud, finishing with the reserved herbs and plenty of cracked pepper and salt flakes.

FRIENDS WITH

Roasted parsnip salad with almond tarator and chermoula p152

With thanks & condiments

Now that you've learned that you *can* make friends with salad, I must tell you about the friends who helped make these salads ... for days!

To Jane Grylls — Grylltown — my food editor and home economist for over a decade, I love the way your brain works, and the way we finish each other's sandwiches. Red dirt, red carpet forever. To Madeleine Dobbins — Dobby — I'm so glad you took a punt and slid into my inbox, and that you roll with anything I throw at you, whether that's a 5 am wake-up for *News Brekkie*, a star-sign inquisition or a retest on a retest on a retest.

To Kirsten Jenkins — KJ — you are so freaking talented, and I'm profoundly grateful that your styling is in this book, and that you're Melbourne's now. Thank you also, for introducing me to photographer Rochelle Eagle, whose EAGLE EYE for light is a genuine gift from the heavens. George Saad, your creativity with design has wrapped the visuals up in a delicious bow. Melody Lord, you've done the same with the words — and taught me to stop generically reminding people to buy Good Quality stuff ... what DOES that even mean? Helena Holmgren, thank you for indexing one of my books for a third time — you help us find the things that need to be found.

To my Murdoch Books fam, you continue to be a steady source of inspiration, support and encouragement, and I am in constant awe of the MB Machine. Publishing director extraordinaire Jane Morrow, head of editorial Virginia Birch, head of creative Megan Pigott, publicists Sarah Hatton and Jemma Crocker-Wilson, and the sales team led by Matt Hoy, Mary-Jayne House, Alice Latham and Britta Martins-Simon OS ... you all hold special places in my heart. Thank you for bringing your brilliance to these books, and for being my publishing village.

To my home village, my chief salad eaters and taste-testers: my family. To Nick and The Nut, thank you for your encouragement, enthusiasm and patience, always. I love cooking with you and for you, and I couldn't ask for a better little tripod to raise me up and keep me stable. To my parents, Frada and Arkady, there's always salad in your fridge and love in your hearts for me, no matter my harebrained ideas. Thank you for instilling in me a love of learning, of teaching, and of VEG! To Stan, my big brother, and to your family too, keep sending me pictures of your cooking, and keep giving me driving pep talks! And of course, to my extended fam, both literally and figuratively, past and present, thank you.

And to you, my fellow enthusiastic eaters and home cooks, thank you for continuing to bring my books into your homes and hearts. Thank you for picking up what I put down, whether that's my writing, my radio and/or telly work, and of course, my books. If you've been a long-time follower of my journey, or met me midstream, thank you for sticking around, for being my penpals, and for amplifying my work by telling your friends about The One with The Glasses, and/or gifting them the fruits of my labour. I look forward to seeing what you cook out of this book!

What to make when you've got ...

Much of salad-making is making salad with what you've got. Combining textures and colours, and bringing them together with a dressing, is about as complex as it needs to get. This ability to riff comes with flying hours (which means this section's got a bit of planned obsolescence built in) but if you're up for some wind beneath your wings, here's a breakdown by veg, so you can reach into the fridge and pull out dinner.

Asparagus

Asparagus and radish salad with caper vinaigrette 126

Asparagus ribbons with pickled pink dressing 92

Skordalia with asparagus and potato peel crisps 96—7

Avocados

Orange veg on green'd quinoa 170—1

Silverbeet & broccoli tumble with herby avocado dressing 220

Tropical prawn salad with archipelago dressing 120

Beans & peas

Baked cauli & feta salad with golden raisin dressing 146—7

Blanch 'n' toss beans 204

Braised flat beans with Svanetia-spiced walnuts 208

Brown-buttered brocc & Brussels with pecorino cloud 225

Charred capsicum on feta & butterbean purée 177

Easy peasy spring salad with parmesan vinaigrette 86

Eggplant and capsicum with fermented black bean dressing 134

Gado gado platter with pantry satay sauce 82—3

Green veg moghrabieh with yoghurt drizzle 70—1

Kipflers and green beans dressed by Almondine 214

Long & short beans with very sharp vinaigrette 36

Miso-roasted cauli with broad bean smash 164—5

Orange veg on green'd quinoa 170—1

Piquant pantry salad with a few green bits 202

Salat olivye 90

Shaved zucchini & edamame salad with pickled ginger 76

SPC long green veg 210

Beetroots

Hot pink pear salad with zippy kale and ricotta 188—9

Roasted beets with spiced walnuts & Georgian garo 187

Shuba salad 192—3

Berries & grapes

Celery and blueberry salad with ranch dressing 124

Hot cheeseboard salad with honey—walnut dressing 130

Pistou-roasted radishes with lentils 142—3

Silverbeet & broccoli tumble with herby avocado dressing 220

Strawberry & rocket salad with peppery parmesan 54

Bitter greens

Asparagus and radish salad with caper vinaigrette 126

Easy peasy spring salad with parmesan vinaigrette 86

Frisée, witlof & grilled fig with goat's cheese 136

Honeyed butternut risoni salad with marinated feta 163

Hot cheeseboard salad with honey–walnut dressing 130

Miso-roasted cauli with broad bean smash 164–5

Pistou-roasted radishes with lentils 142–3

Strawberry & rocket salad with peppery parmesan 54

Tomato tonnato with crispy capers 41

Broccoli, broccolini & cauliflower

Baked cauli & feta salad with golden raisin dressing 146–7

Broccoli and cashew salad-fry 216

Broccolini with self-saucing chickpeas 219

Brown-buttered brocc & Brussels with pecorino cloud 225

Cauli korma crown and cardamom brown rice 178–9

Cauli tabouli with lemony tahini and pomegranate 62

Cypriot salad with pink pickled cauliflower 156–7

Green veg moghrabieh with yoghurt drizzle 70–1

Miso-roasted cauli with broad bean smash 164–5

Silverbeet & broccoli tumble with herby avocado dressing 220

Cabbages

Broccoli and cashew salad-fry 216

Gado gado platter with pantry satay sauce 82–3

Japanese snow slaw with wasabi mayo dressing 56

Orange veg on green'd quinoa 170–1

Rock 'n' roll salad with plum dressing and crispy bits 114

Warm winter slaw with honey & juniper dressing 154

Wombok quick-chi salad 141

Wombok slaw with sweet poppyseed dressing 116

Yampers (camper's jacket yams) 160

Capsicums

Charred capsicum on feta & butterbean purée 177

Eggplant and capsicum with fermented black bean dressing 134

Greek-ish salad with nectarines 42

Piquant pantry salad with a few green bits 202

'Pita lid on it' fattoush salad 102–3

Relaxed chopped salad 80

Squashed squash on yoghurty lemon dressing 34

Tricolour piperade with muffuletta dressing 174

Carrots

3 ways with shredded carrots & daikon 28

Carrot & wild rice salad with marmalade dressing 150

Orange veg on green'd quinoa 170–1

Rock 'n' roll salad with plum dressing and crispy bits 114

Salat olivye 90

Shuba salad 192–3

Warm winter slaw with honey & juniper dressing 154

Yampers (camper's jacket yams) 160

Celery

Celery and blueberry salad with ranch dressing 124

Devilled egg and baby spinach salad 200

Playlunch salad with chilli–honey dressing 122

Citrus

Blanch 'n' toss beans 204

Green mango, pomelo & herb būn 68

Lychee margarita 67

Squashed squash on yoghurty lemon dressing 34

Surf club salad 106

Cucumbers

Cauli tabouli with lemony tahini and pomegranate 62

Cucumber & daikon sheets with tahini–miso dressing 119 ▸▸▸

Cucumber corkscrews with gochujang dressing 78

Gado gado platter with pantry satay sauce 82–3

Greek-ish salad with nectarines 42

Gurkensalat 2.0 95

Honeydew carpaccio with coriander pesto 64

Kind of a big dill 213

'Pita lid on it' fattoush salad 102–3

Relaxed chopped salad 80

Watermelon salad with chilli feta dressing 59

Eggplant

Barbecued adjapsandal with adjika yoghurt dressing 52

Eggplant and capsicum with fermented black bean dressing 134

Eggplant larb with fresh, quickled & fried shallots 48–9

Sticky eggplant, tofu and noodle salad 182

Fennel

Baked cauli & feta salad with golden raisin dressing 146–7

Celery and blueberry salad with ranch dressing 124

Hot pink pear salad with zippy kale and ricotta 188–9

Silverbeet & broccoli tumble with herby avocado dressing 220

Warm winter slaw with honey & juniper dressing 154

Leafy greens

Carrot & wild rice salad with marmalade dressing 150

Devilled egg and baby spinach salad 200

Hot cheeseboard salad with honey–walnut dressing 130

Hot pink pear salad with zippy kale and ricotta 188–9

Playlunch salad with chilli–honey dressing 122

Silverbeet & broccoli tumble with herby avocado dressing 220

Yampers (camper's jacket yams) 160

Lettuce

Bistro bouquet with mignonette dressing 111

Charred corn, cos and tomatoes with paprika–chilli mayo 31

Eggplant larb with fresh, quickled & fried shallots 48–9

Green mango, pomelo & herb būn 68

Grilled cos wedges with anchovy aïoli 112

Mimosa lettuce with retro dressing 100

Scandi breakfast salad 196

Surf club salad 106

Tropical prawn salad with archipelago dressing 120

Olives

Broccolini with self-saucing chickpeas 219

Greek-ish salad with nectarines 42

Piquant pantry salad with a few green bits 202

Potato crack salad with feta crumble 199

Roasted parsnip salad with almond tarator and chermoula 152

Tricolour piperade with muffuletta dressing 174

Watermelon salad with chilli feta dressing 59

Other fruits

Cauli tabouli with lemony tahini and pomegranate 62

Cypriot salad with pink pickled cauliflower 156–7

Frisée, witlof & grilled fig with goat's cheese 136

Fruit salad with zesty dressing and salty–sweet macadamias 67

Green mango, pomelo & herb būn 68

Honeydew carpaccio with coriander pesto 64

Hot pink pear salad with zippy kale and ricotta 188–9

Lychee margarita 67

'Pita lid on it' fattoush salad 102–3

Playlunch salad with chilli–honey dressing 122

Pumpkin wedges with toasty seeds and dill tahini 168

Roasted beets with spiced walnuts & Georgian garo 187

Roasted parsnip salad with almond tarator and chermoula 152

Tropical prawn salad with archipelago dressing 120

Watermelon salad with chilli feta dressing 59

Wombok quick-chi salad 141

Wombok slaw with sweet poppyseed dressing 116

Potatoes, sweet potatoes & yams

Gado gado platter with pantry satay sauce 82–3

Kipflers and green beans dressed by Almondine 214

Potato crack salad with feta crumble 199

Radish & potato salad with creamy tarragon dressing 44

Salat olivye 90

Scandi breakfast salad 196

Shuba salad 192–3

Skordalia with asparagus and potato peel crisps 96–7

Yampers (camper's jacket yams) 160

Pumpkins & butternut squash

Honeyed butternut risoni salad with marinated feta 163

Orange veg on green'd quinoa 170–1

Pumpkin wedges with toasty seeds and dill tahini 168

Radishes & daikon

3 ways with shredded carrots & daikon 28

Asparagus and radish salad with caper vinaigrette 126

Bistro bouquet with mignonette dressing 111

Cucumber & daikon sheets with tahini–miso dressing 119

Devilled egg and baby spinach salad 200

Eggplant larb with fresh, quickled & fried shallots 48–9

Pistou-roasted radishes with lentils 142–3

Radish & potato salad with creamy tarragon dressing 44

Scandi breakfast salad 196

Sprouts & kohlrabi

Agrodolce roasted brassicas with macadamia cream 222

Brown-buttered brocc & Brussels with pecorino cloud 225

Japanese snow slaw with wasabi mayo dressing 56

Stone fruits

Greek-ish salad with nectarines 42

Grilled peach salad with burrata and green peppercorns 60

Triple cherry Caprese with bright basil oil 47

Tomatoes

Barbecued adjapsandal with adjika yoghurt dressing 52

Calamari and shell pasta salad 133

Cauli tabouli with lemony tahini and pomegranate 62

Gado gado platter with pantry satay sauce 82–3

Greek-ish salad with nectarines 42

Honeydew carpaccio with coriander pesto 64

Long & short beans with very sharp vinaigrette 36

'Pita lid on it' fattoush salad 102–3

Relaxed chopped salad 80

Surf club salad 106

Tomato tonnato with crispy capers 41

Triple cherry Caprese with bright basil oil 47

Twinkling tomatoes with milk kefir dressing 32

Zucchinis & summer squash

Barbecued adjapsandal with adjika yoghurt dressing 52

Charred & smashed zucchini with labneh and chilli oil 75

Green veg moghrabieh with yoghurt drizzle 70–1

Sautéed squash and zucchini with pangrattato 26

Shaved zucchini & edamame salad with pickled ginger 76

Squashed squash on yoghurty lemon dressing 34

Index

235

Published in 2024 by Murdoch Books, an imprint of Allen & Unwin

Murdoch Books Australia
Cammeraygal Country
83 Alexander Street
Crows Nest NSW 2065
Phone: +61 (0)2 8425 0100
murdochbooks.com.au
info@murdochbooks.com.au

Murdoch Books UK
Ormond House
26–27 Boswell Street
London WC1N 3JZ
Phone: +44 (0) 20 8785 5995
murdochbooks.co.uk
info@murdochbooks.co.uk

For corporate orders and custom publishing, contact our business development team at salesenquiries@murdochbooks.com.au

Publisher: Jane Morrow
Editorial manager: Virginia Birch
Head of creative: Megan Pigott
Designer: George Saad
Editor: Melody Lord
Photographer: Rochelle Eagle
Stylist: Kirsten Jenkins
Food editor: Jane Grylls
Home economist: Madeleine Dobbins
Production director: Lou Playfair

Text © Alice Zaslavsky 2024
The moral right of the author has been asserted.
Design © Murdoch Books 2024
Photography © Rochelle Eagle 2024

SCAN HERE FOR EVEN MORE
VEG-FORWARD RECIPES

Murdoch Books acknowledges the Traditional Owners of the Country on which we live and work. We pay our respects to all Aboriginal and Torres Strait Islander Elders, past and present.

ISBN 978 1 92261 677 7

 A catalogue record for this book is available from the National Library of Australia

A catalogue record for this book is available from the British Library

Colour reproduction by Splitting Image Colour Studio Pty Ltd, Wantirna, Victoria
Printed by 1010 Printing International Limited, China

OVEN GUIDE: You may find cooking times vary depending on the oven you are using. For fan-forced ovens, as a general rule, set the oven temperature to 20°C (35°F) lower than indicated in the recipe.

TABLESPOON MEASURES: We have used 20 ml (4 teaspoon) tablespoon measures. If you are using a 15 ml (3 teaspoon) tablespoon add an extra teaspoon of the ingredient for each tablespoon specified.

10 9 8 7 6 5 4 3